Praise for
Wisdom Meets Passion

"My friend Dan Miller has been teaching people how to discover their life's calling for more than twenty years, and his best student just may be his son Jared Angaza. These two guys are as different as night and day, but when you combine Dan's old-school wisdom with Jared's cutting-edge passion, you get a solid, comprehensive plan for attacking your life and career goals."

> — **Dave Ramsey**, New York
> Times best-selling author and
> nationally syndicated radio show
> host

"The message presented in this book leaves the door open to two dangerous outcomes. The first is that readers might not take it seriously and continue their lives of mediocrity, thinking small and dismissing the truth held in their hands, thereby denying a surefire call to live out the fullness of who they were created to be. The second and far more dangerous risk is that they believe what is offered here and embark on a journey that drastically alters their lives and the lives of countless others. It won't be safe. It won't be secure. Not by the world's standards. But it will be epic. It will be worthy. It will be true. Either way, it's a risk. Which will you choose?"

> — **Kevin Miller**, proud son of Dan,
> honored brother of Jared, and
> grateful founder of Free Agent
> Academy

"What is more important, wisdom or passion? According to Dan Miller and Jared Angaza, both. They make the brilliant case that you can't succeed in today's world—let alone be satisfied—by focusing on one at the expense of the other. Thankfully, they show us how to get more of each, using their unique generational perspectives to add depth and texture to the journey."

> — **Michael Hyatt**, author, Platform:
> Get Noticed in a Noisy World

message of *Wisdom Meets Passion* is not only inspiring; it is pow-
~ully effective. If you want abundance—in terms of meaning and
~noney—read Dan and Jared's book, and apply what you learn. Your
life will be richer for it."

— **Erin Casey**, books editor,
Success magazine; and author,
Zany Zia's Hats to Where series.

"Dan and Jared masterfully illuminate the need for finding and
releasing the wisdom and passion in each of us, thus leading to an
extraordinary life. Whether you are eighteen or eighty, you'll benefit
from the principles laid out here."

— **Ken Abraham**, *New York Times*
best-selling author

"I've known Dan for nearly two decades, and I've never failed to notice
that sparkle in his eye—the result of an explosive mix of wisdom *and*
passion. He's got it, and I highly recommend you learn from him. You
will never be the same."

— **Ed Smith, PhD**, president,
Williamson Christian College

"There must be a balance between accumulating knowledge and developing fulfilling relationships. This book will be especially helpful to
employers hiring, training, and promoting generation Y employees."

— **Jack Faris**, president/CEO,
National Federation of
Independent Business (NFIB),
retired

"I can't think of better guides than Dan and his son Jared to illuminate
both sides of the same coin. Passion and wisdom bridge the chasm of
generational perspectives that needlessly separate us."

— **Jeff Moseley**, president,
FairTrade Services

"None of us wants to live a mediocre life. In this book Dan and Jared shine light on the exciting process of blending wisdom and passion for a born-to-win life. If you are ready to really live the life you were born to have, then this book is a must for you."

— **Tom Ziglar**, CEO, Ziglar Inc.

"Wisdom provides the daily insight you need to make it for the long-haul. Passion is the love required to live and work with excellence. These two powerful engines never produce alone what they create together. Dan and Jared demonstrate this beautiful harmony as father and son, wisdom and passion, and provide a grand invitation for cross-generational enterprise."

— **Wes Yoder**, author, *Bond of Brothers*

"*Wisdom Meets Passion* is an artful approach to life, business, philanthropy, and authentic success. I have personally witnessed Jared's passion and results-oriented humanitarianism in Africa. And I have experienced Dan's provocative wisdom through his paradigm-shifting books. Here we get the best of both. A must-read for anyone who cares about creating a better world for themselves and others."

— **Pastor Terry A. Smith**, TheLifeChristianChurch

"Dan and Jared brilliantly weave the explanation behind the compelling equation that sculpts your life. All You've Learned from Your Past + Your Dreams, Passions, and Plans for Your Future = How You Can Succeed Today."

— **Rabbi Daniel Lapin**, author, *Thou Shall Prosper*

"It's not just about wisdom and passion—this inspiring book redefines security for multiple generations, offering clear steps, surprising examples, and hope. This book will change the world!"

— **Chris Guillebeau**, author, *The $100 Startup*

"*Wisdom Meets Passion* provides a unique and refreshing perspective regarding what being successful really means. It challenges one to be introspective and chart a course of success based on personal goals with regard to a purposeful life; rather than materialistic societal definitions of success."

— **Gretchen H. Campbell, MD**,
medical business consultant and
author, *Doc-Preneur*

"*Wisdom Meets Passion* is one of those books that I will read over and over again. Both writers have told their stories in an honest, loving, artistic light. This is the kind of read you want to give to everyone you love."

— **Dorsey McHugh**, artist, Step
into the Story

"Brilliantly done. The father and son writing team weave together a modern-day classic. Jared's raw emotion and expressive writing style are a wonderful compliment to the tried-and-true messages that are always part of Dan Miller's writings."

— **Joel Boggess**, author, *Passion:
4 places you forgot to look*;
www.powerfulliving.tv

"Contained within the covers of this book is the quote that will change your life! Whether you're in need of fresh inspiration . . . new direction . . . or the gumption to begin what you've always dreamed but never dared, this book will serve you. In a literary world of How-to monologues, this book stands apart as a Why-to conversation about the stuff that makes life matter. If you've been looking for the book that will pull you out of the mire of monotony and into the fray of impassioned living, you found it!"

— **Bill Spencer**, executive director,
Narrow Gate Foundation

WISDOM

MEETS

PASSION

When Generations
Collide and Collaborate

Dan Miller *and* **Jared Angaza**

THOMAS NELSON
Since 1798

NASHVILLE   DALLAS   MEXICO CITY   RIO DE JANEIRO

Published in Nashville, Tennessee, by Thomas Nelson. Thomas Nelson is a registered trademark of Thomas Nelson, Inc.

Thomas Nelson, Inc., titles may be purchased in bulk for educational, business, fund-raising, or sales promotional use. For information, please e-mail SpecialMarkets@ThomasNelson.com.

Unless otherwise noted, Scripture quotations are taken from *The Living Bible.* © 1971. Used by permission of Tyndale House Publishers, Inc., Wheaton, Illinois 60189. All rights reserved.

Scripture quotations marked NIV are taken from the Holy Bible, New International Version®, NIV®. Copyright © 1973, 1978, 1984, 2011 by Biblica, Inc.™ Used by permission of Zondervan. All rights reserved worldwide. www.zondervan.com.

Scripture quotations marked MSG are taken from *The Message* by Eugene H. Peterson. © 1993, 1994, 1995, 1996, 2000. 2001, 2002. Used by permission of NavPress Publishing Group.

Scripture quotations marked NKJV are taken from the New King James Version®. © 1982 by Thomas Nelson, Inc. Used by permission. All rights reserved.

Scripture quotations marked GNT are taken from the Good News Translation. © 1976, 1992 by The American Bible Society. Used by permission. All rights reserved.

Scripture quotations marked KJV are taken from the King James Version.

Scripture quotations marked NLT are taken from the *Holy Bible*, New Living Translation. © 1996, 2004, 2007. Used by permission of Tyndale House Publishers, Inc., Wheaton, Illinois 60189. All rights reserved.

Chad Jeffers photograph (chapter 4) © Sara Rose Photograph. Used by permission.

ISBN 978-0-8499-4846-6 (HC)

Library of Congress Cataloging-in-Publication Data

Miller, Dan, 1937–
  Wisdom meets passion : when generations collide and collaborate / Dan Miller and Jared Angaza.
    p. cm.
  Includes bibliographical references.
  ISBN 978-0-8499-4742-1 (trade paper)
  1. Self-realization. 2. Conduct of life. 3. Wisdom. 4. Success in business. 5. Success.
6. Miller, Dan, 1937- I. Angaza, Jared. II. Title.
  BF637.S4M5474 2012
  650.1—dc23   2012011420

Printed in the United States of America

12 13 14 15 16 17 QG 6 5 4 3 2 1

To our wives, Joanne and Ilea,

who inspire us daily as they exemplify
the blending of wisdom and passion.

You both foster a safe environment
of love and support for us to dream,
experiment, and open new doors for
living an extraordinary life. We are who
we are because of you. Much love.

Contents

Preface   x

Introduction   xii

Chapter One: I Just Want to Make a Difference   1
Chapter Two: Where Do I Find Security?   33
Chapter Three: I Owe $133,000 and Can't Find a Job   55
Chapter Four: Lemonade Stand or Facebook   87
Chapter Five: Doing Work That Matters   115
Chapter Six: Who Are You, and Why Are You Here?   133
Chapter Seven: I Asked for Wonder   157
Chapter Eight: Not (Only) for Profit   189
Chapter Nine: Retirement: The American Dream?   205
Chapter Ten: I Have a Feeling We're Not in Kansas Anymore   219

Acknowledgments   234

Notes   237

About the Authors   256

Preface

Baby boomers have relied on wisdom to pave the way to success. Education, knowledge, investing strategies, 401(k)s, real estate leverage, and carefully contrived career paths were expected to lead to success in one's golden years. Seeing the overall failure of that formulaic approach to life, younger generations today have relied on passion as the guiding principle for their version of success. Just find something cool to do; forget having a mortgage and a BMW in the driveway.

And yet both are necessary. Regardless of age, those using only wisdom to achieve their goals are likely to end up disappointed and unfulfilled—feeling as though they have been chasing empty rainbows. Those trusting passion alone may lose the power of wisdom and end up underachieving, falling short of their potential and unable to attain their worthy goals.

Wisdom without passion can feel like having that BMW in the driveway with no gas in the tank. And passion without wisdom can appear as a tricked-out 1957 Chevy with no steering wheel. *Wisdom Meets Passion* will show you how to blend the two—equipping you to accomplish your greatest financial goals, experience the thrill of fulfilling relationships, create meaningful work, and complete your purpose and calling here on earth no matter which age group you represent.

Introduction

T his book is about the different generational approaches to
work, money, education—well, just about everything in
life. I (Dan) was raised in a very traditional, rural, hardwork-
ing, legalistic environment. My dad was the pastor of a small
Mennonite church, so we farmed as a way to generate meager
funds for survival. I was expected to be responsible, get good
grades in school, and then join my dad in the farming operation.
There was no talk of having a purpose or of finding work that
was fulfilling. We were responsible and did whatever was practical and realistic.

Jared is my second child. He seemed to push the boundaries
of being normal from the moment of birth. When he was two
years old, his mom and I resorted to using a soft cloth to tie his
leg to the side of his crib because he would just get up and wan-
der around the house at all hours of the night. When he was five
and six, he dressed up like Mr. T and was not opposed to wearing scarves, earrings, and makeup. By the time he reached the
sixth grade, his mother and I knew we had a unique opportunity to find an environment other than a regular classroom for

Jared. It was clear he could not or would not be confined to such a predictable setting. We elected to homeschool in an attempt to maintain some semblance of an academic path and to secure an alternate high school diploma. As we observed how his mind worked, we included arts, hands-on mechanics, and auditory teaching in all subjects. We used time-outs of listening to motivational speakers like Zig Ziglar, Brian Tracy, and Mark Victor Hansen to shape his thinking and release his uniqueness. Jared sought adventure and danger rather than safety. He seemed to welcome risk and uncertainty rather than predictability. Instead of following the path of my traditional education, he wanted experience. While he participated in any religious services we attended, he also questioned any accepted belief and went deep into new possibilities.

Today, at thirty-three years old, Jared lives in Mombasa, Kenya, with his beautiful wife, Ilea. They have adopted a Rwandan boy named Francois, who had been living on the streets of Kigali. Jared has an uncanny ability to find opportunities to create more than ample income—and adventure, meaningful relationships, and awesome experiences—for his growing family. With hearts for Africa they decided to change their surname to better reflect the culture they call home. Thus you see father and son: Dan Miller and Jared Angaza. Jared and Ilea took the Swahili surname *Angaza*, which means "to bring light." Yes, his mom and I were supportive of that decision, as we are of all the things that allow Jared to be fully alive.

We want to share our stories—not with the expectation that you will duplicate our lives but as a way for you to see into lives that are dramatically different in observable details yet strikingly similar in values and heart issues. As you read these pages, it is our hope that you will take a fresh look at your principles and lifestyle and perhaps those of your children, your parents, your neighbors, or the people living on the other side of the world. Our desire is not that you question valued traditions but that you would perhaps be more open to acceptance of people whose experiences may be different from your own.

As a baby boomer I tend to look at life as one long linear story. Members of Jared's generation view their lives more as continuing chapters—not as one long novel. They can try one path, experience it as good or bad, and then start a new chapter.

I have been coaching people through career changes for more than twenty years. It has been in walking through real-life transitions that the concepts and principles presented here have been developed. Today I continue to write, speak, and coach under the umbrella of 48Days.com. (The 48 Days comes from establishing a reasonable time frame in which to make any life change—to avoid procrastination and quickly move to positive action.)

While I wrote the original content, we essentially present the ideas here as one voice, integrating wisdom and passion and the perspectives of two widely different generations. Jared then added his personal thoughts to expand selected issues. You'll see those thoughts in **dark-orange** print. The examples in this book originated with real situations encountered by those I've met through speaking, coaching, or the intersections of our lives. For some of my sources, I am protecting their anonymity. In those cases I've created fictional names that appear in quotation marks.

We assume wisdom comes with age and passion is the exciting trait of the young. But as you will see unfolding in the chapters, wisdom is found in abundance in those who are very young and passion is a strong characteristic of those who continue living lives that matter. Expect both to be expanded in your life as you share this journey with us.

I Just Want to Make a Difference

My earliest recollection of having and acting on a dream happened when I was a ten-year-old farm kid in Ohio. My mom had canned and frozen all the sweet corn needed to provide for our family of seven for the coming year. But I saw the remaining ears of corn in that big garden and those that were continuing to fill out. With Dad's permission I got up early one morning and began picking those big, juicy ears of corn. I filled the little red trailer I had connected behind our Ford tractor. With the trailer bursting with those ears still covered by the morning dew, I drove the two miles up the dirt road to where it intersected with the paved road that headed into town. I parked so all traffic could easily see me, and I set up my little sign: "Fresh Sweet Corn—$.30 Dozen." And thus I was introduced to the world of providing a product and expecting a fair exchange of money.

I was captured by the adrenaline rush of running my own business. People loved my sweet corn, and I loved getting their money. That thrill of providing something of value in exchange for a few coins has never diminished. But I realized even then that money by itself has no value—only when the exchange continues does the process of commerce have meaning. And very early on I wanted to do something that made a difference.

Do you remember your childhood dreams? All ten-year-olds know how to dream. You know the typical fantasies. They can dream of becoming a firefighter, astronaut, ship captain, artist, or rock star. But then life happens. Some of those kids were told their dreams were unrealistic. You may have been one of those kids. Somewhere along the way you were taught to be realistic, to stay inside the lines and recognize that growing up means you need to show up at eight o'clock and go home to a dreary existence at five o'clock.

Have you allowed your dreams to be washed away by the big wave called Life? Is it really too late to create a plan of action to bring your dreams to reality? What can you do today to act on a dream that's been languishing in those precious childlike recesses of your mind?

There are two great days in our lives—the day we are born and the day we discover *why*.
—WILLIAM BARCLAY[1]

Can you identify both of those days in your life?

So what are you doing with your dreams? Did the dreams you had two years ago change the life you have today?

The old American Dream defined *success* as a stable job, a great paycheck with benefits, a house in the suburbs, and a secure retirement plan. With all of those items now in jeopardy, the search has become more philosophical and spiritual. Today I hear people saying, "I just want to do something noble, humanitarian, or socially responsible. I just want to make a difference."

To dream alone is fantasy if it doesn't move the heart to act.

—DAN ALLENDER[2]

Fortunately I was raised in a family that encouraged me to dream big and follow that dream. We were taught that anything is possible. With that belief, I've traveled all over the United States and spent the last six years living in East Africa.

I started my first business at thirteen years old. At that point I'd spent my life racing BMX bikes with my father and brother. We were at the top of our game, and we absolutely loved racing. Consequently, I knew a lot about the mechanics of a bike.

So I started my own neighborhood bicycle repair company. I put flyers on mailboxes and offered free pickup and delivery (by foot). Over the course of a summer, I made my first five hundred dollars. I used that to put toward my first car.

I had been enthralled with Africa since I was six years old, directly after seeing the first *We Are the World* music video hosted by Michael Jackson. My love of Africa grew exponentially from that day.

When I was sixteen, I started studying Mombasa, Kenya. I wanted so badly to be in Africa, where the life is raw and so much of the landscape is untainted by the need for mass consumption. I wanted to live on the Swahili Coast, where the primary concern is fostering relationships and appreciating the earth and the life that God created for us.

People thought my little dream was cute. But I studied, believed, and worked hard for it. Now I'm here, living with my wife and our adopted Rwandan son; our first baby is on the way.

Climbing the Pyramid or Skipping to the Top

Remember the pyramid on the opposite page from your introductory psychology class? Abraham Maslow determined that we can track people through a logical progression from the bottom to the top of the pyramid. People are concerned about their physiological needs first. If someone is hungry, he isn't concerned about saving the world—that person is going to be looking for something to eat. If someone doesn't have a safe place to stay, that will be her primary concern. It's only after basic needs have been taken care of that anyone can climb up to the top of the pyramid—self-actualization or even transcendence, wanting to be part of something that goes beyond himself or herself. But wait a minute. Is that really the way it always happens? Do you know anyone who has seemingly ignored his own needs with a higher desire to help someone else?

MASLOW'S HIERARCHY OF NEEDS

TRANSCENDENCE
Being part of something larger than self

SELF-ACTUALIZATION
Using best skills, talents, passions and dreams

ESTEEM NEEDS
Feeling of being appreciated and honored

BELONGING AND LOVE NEEDS
Intimate relationships, friends

SAFETY NEEDS
Safe place, security

BASIC NEEDS
Food, water, warmth, rest

Ever heard of Mother Teresa? How about these people?

Maggie Gobran is a Coptic Christian from Egypt, who founded the charity organization Stephen's Children Ministry in Mokattam, outside Cairo, Egypt. She said, "When I touch a poor child, I'm touching Jesus. When I listen to a poor child, I'm listening to God's heart for all of humanity."[3]

Somaly Mam is a Cambodian author and human rights advocate, focusing primarily on needs of victims of human sex trafficking. She has garnered official and media acclaim for her efforts.[4]

Nelson Mandela is one of the greatest examples of bucking the concepts that Maslow put forth. Mandela spent twenty-seven years in prison, just to prove a point!

When Jared was a teenager, we, as parents, would make him empty his pockets before going to downtown Nashville with his friends for the evening. We knew whatever he had he would give away before coming home. Not that it would be spent on candy or trinkets for himself. Rather he would give it to people who obviously needed it more than he did. One Christmas I carefully selected a really cool leather jacket I knew he would love. A couple nights later I noticed he came home without it. Upon questioning, Jared simply shared that he saw a guy with no coat. He knew he had several more at home, so why wouldn't he give it to someone who had none?

Many, especially in the younger generation today, seem to ignore Maslow's carefully defined pyramid. They ignore their basic needs to move up the pyramid all the way to transcendence (being involved in something that goes beyond the created world). The desire to make a difference is a stronger pull than having another bag of Doritos or even a BMW.

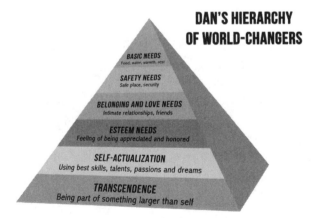

DAN'S HIERARCHY OF WORLD-CHANGERS

BASIC NEEDS
Food, water, warmth, rest

SAFETY NEEDS
Safe place, security

BELONGING AND LOVE NEEDS
Intimate relationships, friends

ESTEEM NEEDS
Feeling of being appreciated and honored

SELF-ACTUALIZATION
Using best skills, talents, passions and dreams

TRANSCENDENCE
Being part of something larger than self

We'll find this to be an ongoing issue in those who blend passion and wisdom. Regardless of where they are on the chronological timeline, they seem to ignore the natural progression of securing one's own needs before being drawn into serving others.

So many people in my generation were raised to believe that Maslow's hierarchy of needs was the only formula for success. While I certainly believe he had some valid points for the masses, I also believe he neglected to incorporate people who govern their lives from a more altruistic foundation.

There are a lot of rules that the Western world has created in order to maintain control and order. Time and money tend to be the premise for most of them. But I view time, money, and dogmatic religion as coping mechanisms created by man. In the short term it's easier to create hierarchies and controlling mechanisms. However, historically, those systems have never been sustainable, nor do they tend to incite true happiness.

I never really cared about having nice things or even having food on my table. I have always chosen relationships over comfort or material things. Consequently, I've lived a life of deep, meaningful relationships. People often comment on the fact that I am still so close to the boys I grew up with. Now that we're all grown up, we're still like brothers, and I've been friends with most of them for nearly twenty years. They are family that I chose.

Those relationships mean more to me than anything I could ever achieve on my own. I'd rather be hungry with a friend than have a full belly on my own. That will never change.

I don't remember to whom I gave that jacket, but I do remember giving it away. I remember how I felt after having done it. I've carried that feeling with me ever since. It has nothing to do with my comfort levels, money, or the status quo. It has everything to do with true human connection. It can't be bought, traded, or leveraged. It's as pure as you get.

To each there comes in their lifetime a special moment when they are figuratively tapped on the shoulder and offered the chance to do a very special thing, unique to them and fitted to their talents. What a tragedy if that moment finds them unprepared or unqualified for that which could have been their finest hour.

—WINSTON S. CHURCHILL[5]

Can you identify your special moment when you were "tapped on the shoulder," or are you still waiting?

Are you prepared and qualified for that moment?

If Brad Can Do It, I Can Too

At the beginning of each year, we all think about setting big goals. And rightfully so. I encourage you to think big. But don't get stuck hoping to be the next Taylor Swift when you're not willing to play tonight's gig down at the local pizza shop. Most famous people started with not-so-famous work experiences.

Check these out:

Donald Trump, now an ultrarich real estate investor, got his start collecting soda bottles for the deposit money.[6]

Michael Dell, founder of Dell Computers, washed dishes at a Chinese restaurant before hitting it big with his computers.[7]

Johnny Depp donned makeup for his gig in a KISS tribute

band as a young performer. Back then he often made about $25 a night; today he makes much more than $25 million a year.[8]

Chris Rock started his career as a busboy at a Red Lobster in Queens, New York. His first jokes included, "The thing about Red Lobster is that if you work there, you can't afford to eat there. You're making minimum wage. A shrimp cost minimum wage."[9]

Lucille Ball was reportedly fired from an ice-cream shop for not remembering to add bananas to banana splits. Her famous skit in which she struggled to wrap candies from the conveyor belt that kept speeding up came out of those early days in food service.[10]

Tom Hanks started out as a popcorn-and-peanuts vendor at the Oakland Coliseum in California. Then he worked his way up to a hotel bellhop, carrying bags for the stars.[11]

Madonna worked at Dunkin' Donuts as a teenager. Today, as one of the richest celebrities in the world, she could buy all the doughnuts she wants.[12]

Brad Pitt drove limos, moved refrigerators, and dressed up as a chicken trying to convince customers to visit a Mexican restaurant.[13]

Mariah Carey was a beauty school dropout. Then she was fired from her job as a hat checker. Today she's one of the most successful female vocalists of all time.[14]

Embrace the work opportunity you have today. It may be the stepping-stone you need on your way to success. No one goes from having a dream to fame and fortune overnight. As I've already mentioned, when I was a ten-year-old, I sold sweet corn on the side of the road for thirty cents a dozen. In high school I earned extra money cleaning out chicken coops on the weekends. The chicken waste I was shoveling created an ammonia smell that burned my eyes and nose. It was nasty, stinky, backbreaking work. But those jobs taught me the value of hard work and provided the incentive to look for better options.

What's the one job that sticks out in your journey of getting to where you are today? And what was the lesson you learned?

Steven Spielberg reportedly once warned, "Good ideas are only given to you for a limited amount of time. If you don't act on them, they belong to someone else."

Wow! Do you think you've missed an idea by not acting on it?

And speaking of celebrities who want to make a difference:

WHO NEEDS CELEBRITY PHILANTHROPY?

The masses continuously lambast the likes of Angelina Jolie,[15] Brad Pitt, and Bono,[16] complaining about their incessant philanthropic focus and how it only bolsters their careers.

Why are these celebrities using their star power to generate millions of dollars for charity and garner backing from influential political leaders when they could just keep buying Ferraris and houses in the Hamptons? It's madness!

What?

When was the last time you dedicated even a fraction of your time, money, or influence toward a philanthropic endeavor, much less countless hours and millions of dollars?

What are you doing right now to make the world a better, more peaceful, and loving place?

When was the last time you honed your musical talent, created a successful rock band, and dropped $32 billion in debt from eighteen African countries or raised more money and awareness for eradicating HIV in Africa than any other human on the planet? Bono does that in his spare time. Literally.

George Clooney recently launched the Satellite Sentinel Project,[17] designed to deter mass atrocities and crimes against humanity in Sudan and South Sudan. I've been volunteering and lobbying for this kind of effort in that region for almost ten years. Clooney put this together in less than a year, and it's one of the most effective philanthropic initiatives I've ever witnessed. Phenomenal.

Pitt and Jolie have given millions of dollars to philanthropy. Jolie has spent serious amounts of time in more than twenty-two poverty-stricken countries, purchased fleets of airplanes, acted as a UNHCR ambassador, flown into extreme threat zones when others wouldn't, and much more. Pitt and Jolie donated $8 million in 2006 alone.[18]

In December 2001, Perry Farrell, who is the front man for Jane's Addiction and creator of Lollapalooza, flew into politically troubled Sudan with other members of Christian Solidarity International to negotiate the release of Sudanese slaves.[19] Jane's Addiction donated its earnings from one concert for the redemption of more than twenty-three hundred people. Most parents wouldn't let their kids listen to this rock star.

I could go on and on. The list of philanthropic celebrities is endless. I've only touched on a few, largely because they are the ones most criticized.

Is there anyone who can look at this list, along with thousands of other instances, and say that this work shouldn't have been done? Is their work irrelevant because they are famous?

Do these celebrities gain more power and money because of their good deeds? They sure do. Why shouldn't they? It just gives them more power and more money to do more good.

There are plenty of celebs out there just using their power for personal gain. If you want to gripe about celebrities, how about putting the negative focus on the self-centered ones?

How hypocritical and dichotomous is it for people to criticize celebs for doing good around the world? Who cares what they gain from it? What I care about is the fact that so much good is being done in such a public manner that it's creating a new standard and trend. Can you think of a better trend to foster?

Seriously. Why would you fight a trend of famous, influential rich people donating their time and money to philanthropy? Really?

Who needs celebrity philanthropy? The world does. In fact, we could use a little philanthropy from anyone willing to do it well, don't you think?

When You Have Nothing . . .

Every year my wife, Joanne, and I go to Chicago for our annual pre-Christmas excursion. The weather is often bitterly cold, and the streets are bustling with the usual last-minute shoppers. And as usual, the sidewalks typically have all too many people with quickly constructed cardboard signs, hoping to capture the sympathy of passing shoppers.

I saw one sign that said:

> Lost my Job
> Lost my Home
> Lost my Hope
> Please Help

What's the next step? Is this really an inevitable sequence? Does our hope disappear if we don't have a job or a home? Are we that dependent on favorable circumstances?

I was reading about the inventions that are coming out of the slums of Nairobi, Kenya. The tagline on the story said, "When you have nothing, anything is possible."[20]

If circumstances control our hope, we are most vulnerable. Hope or optimism is not about denying reality; it's about seeing the possibilities for creating a better reality than you currently have. Yes, I've always been accused of being a glass-half-full kind of guy because I really do believe that every problem brings with it the seed of a solution, and I believe that the search for a solution can itself be inspiring and hopeful. If you lose hope, you will not be looking for solutions and will miss them even if they pass right in front of your nose.

More can be gained by focusing on those talents and gifts you know God has given you. Focus on what you're moving to, not what you're moving *from*. Circumstances beyond your control may lead to losing your job and maybe your home, but losing hope is a choice. Remember, "When you have nothing, anything is possible."

Twenty years from now, you will be more
disappointed by the things that you didn't do than
by the ones you did do. So throw off the bowlines.
Sail away from the safe harbor. Catch the trade
winds in your sails. Explore. Dream. Discover.

—MARK TWAIN[21]

Start with what you have. If you wait until you have the confidence you need to do a job search, the education you need before you're a great candidate, or the money you need to start a business, you'll never start anything. Start today. Start walking toward your ultimate success.

What are you doing this year that you were afraid to attempt last year? If you're doing only the same things, you'll get the same results.

What Are You Gonna Be?

When you get to heaven, God is not going to ask you why you weren't more like Mother Teresa, Billy Graham, or Bono. He's likely to ask you why you weren't more like you. Your responsibility and source of real freedom and success are to discover who you are. Lead with your unique talents and personality. Be authentically you, and let God use you.

Remember the 1994 movie *Forrest Gump*? At one part, Jenny asks, "What are you gonna be when you grow up?" and Forrest replies, "Why can't I be me?" That's your challenge—be authentically you.

Theologian Frederick Buechner once told a graduating class:

The voice we should listen to most as we choose a vocation is the voice that we might think we should listen to least, and that is the voice of our own gladness. What can we do that makes us the gladdest, what can we do that leaves us with the strongest sense of sailing true north . . . ? Is it making things with our hands out of wood or stone or paint or canvas? Or is it making something we hope like truth out of words? Or is it making people laugh or weep in a way that cleanses their spirit? I believe that if it is a thing that makes us truly glad, then it is a good thing and it is our thing and it is the calling voice that we were made to answer with our lives.[22]

A tree gives glory to God by being a tree. For in being what God means it to be it is obeying Him. . . . The more a tree is like itself, the more it is like Him.

—**THOMAS MERTON**[23]

Can you trust what makes you glad? Could that really be the voice of your calling? Are you willing to do what makes you glad, or do you think that would be self-serving? Do you know that when you're doing something that gives you pleasure, you do it with more energy and enthusiasm than when trying to do something just because you think it's right, godly, humanitarian, or honorable?

Don't be guilty of this . . .

I spent much of my life trying to be Bono or Nelson Mandela or Mother Teresa. I've always been driven to bring more love, peace, and equality to the world, and naturally these iconic humanitarians have inspired me through their lives.

But it wasn't until I discovered my own talents and embraced them that I began to actually make a positive impact. I did some nice things along the way, but I didn't gain any traction until I found peace in the journey of discovering who God created me to be.

God gave me these gifts for a reason. But it's my choice to acknowledge them, hone them, practice them, grow them, and use them for good. Or I could spend my life on a futile mission to become someone else.

My Life Is Too Small

In preparation for 48 Days life coaching, each candidate completes an information profile.[24] A thirty-six-year-old MBA in a high-level executive position shared this concern in her advance information: "I have a vague sense that my life is too small."

Living large does not necessarily mean a bigger salary, house, cars, or retirement fund. It has nothing to do with fancy vacations or the latest fashions. Rather, it means having a life that is full of meaning and purpose. And that can occur—or be absent—at any place on the continuum of the traditional parameters of success. I've seen millionaires who are living life "small" and those with scarce financial resources who are living "large."

Let me ask you this: What is your life saying to the world? Are you living your life too small? Is it so full of meaningless tasks that there's no room left for the things that make your heart sing? Are you pushing so hard in *doing* more that you've lost the sense of *being* more? Does more activity really equal greater accomplishment, or does it at some point tip the scale and begin to diminish the meaning of your life? Are you creating the legacy you want to leave for your loved ones?

Reflect on last month. Yes, just this last month. What did you do to keep your life from being too small?

Can you identify

1. four or five ideas you had for a better job or starting your own business?
2. three things that you did just to help someone out with no expectation of payback?
3. the books you read or listened to that enlightened your spirit, confidence, knowledge, and wisdom?
4. the number of hours you spent in quiet contemplation?
5. two or three things you did that you had never done before?
6. the concerts, art exhibits, seminars, workshops, or other enriching experiences you had?
7. two or three specific things you did to strengthen the relationships that mean the most to you?

If you have no responses to these seven questions, chances are strong that you are living your life too small.

Make it a regular practice to embrace living large times in your life. Wisdom, peace, contentment, and insight about investing your life in fulfilling work will grow in those times. Take a walk; give thanks for simple things; take a bath with music playing and candles burning; turn off the telephone, TV, and computer. Carve out times for restoration and spiritual breathing. Don't confuse activity with accomplishment. Even Jesus got away from the crowds periodically. *Don't let your life be too small.*

I was recently discussing the concept of perspective with my adopted son, Francois, as we sat on our rooftop under the night sky. I explained that our perspective is something we actively choose, every second of the day.

Many people view our life as crazy, irresponsible, simple, and even futile. We don't have much money, we live in a relatively dangerous area in Africa, we take big risks, and we are about as unorthodox as one can be. We are not living the American Dream of having a big house with lots of stuff and being normal. The perspective of many people is that we are not living a successful life.

Francois asked me why we don't strive to be rich. I said, "We *are* rich! We have an amazing family, a beautiful rooftop view of the Indian Ocean, and meaningful relationships with family and friends. We are not governed by fear, and our lives are full of love. We are not hungry or wanting, and we are not weighed down by loads of material things. We are free, and we are blessed."

Money and things will always come and go throughout life. I am grateful that we have a roof over our heads and food to eat every day. I am grateful that we have the basic things we need. But our wealth is in our relationships and our perspectives. We don't subscribe to the same rules and standards as much of the Western world, and we never will.

Our lifestyle is our choice, every moment of every day. And from my perspective, we are richer than anyone else I know. Our destiny is a choice, not a jail sentence. Francois now has the power to choose his life. He is no longer ignorant of that possibility.

In our family, we find our wealth in relationships. So

we spend our days fostering great friendships and showing love to everyone we encounter. I think that makes our
lives *large*.

Are You a Doofus?

As a young boy, Norman Vincent Peale thought he lacked brains
and ability. In one of his many books he wrote, "I constantly
told myself that I had no brains, no ability; that I didn't amount
to anything and never would. . . . I then became aware that
people were agreeing with me; for it is a fact that others will
unconsciously take you at your own self-appraisal."[25] A college
professor said he was "disgusted" with Peale and asked him,
"Why do you go skulking through life like a scared rabbit?"

Working through his own challenging feelings of inferiority
led Dr. Peale to write *The Power of Positive Thinking*, his best-
known book that has now sold more than twenty million copies.

What is holding you back? T. Harv Eker, author of *Secrets of
the Millionaire Mind*, says we all have a "money blueprint."[26] Here's
how it seems to work. We all have a certain level of achievement
we think we deserve. If a person gets over that level momentarily,
it's not uncommon to see that person subconsciously *under-
achieve* to regain the success level he believed was his limit.

I see this as people are looking for a new job. If they have
been making $40,000, they will look at jobs in the $35,000 to
$45,000 range. If a position is available that fits their skill set
perfectly and pays $75,000, they often don't even apply. Their
level of belief or of deserving doesn't match that level of reward.
Look at what happens to most lottery winners. Within about
three years most are right back at their previous level of having nothing. Their unexpected wealth didn't match their sense

of deserving, and they made the adjustments to bring things back into sync. Look at NFL football players Pacman Jones and Plaxico Burress—they sabotaged their millions to match the real world as they see it.

I see a whole lot of confusing theology in this arena. Is it more godly to expect riches or to be content with poverty? While space does not allow a full treatment of that hot potato here, rest assured that your beliefs in that area are likely evident in your reality. If you think you deserve poverty, your world will line up to confirm that belief. If you think you are the child of the King and have access to unlimited resources, your reality will likely confirm that. Circumstances, however, do not determine your well-being. If you think you're a doofus,[27] your world will confirm the truth of your belief. This is very much a head and a heart issue. Be careful of the messages you're telling yourself and others.

> Consult not your fears but your hopes and
> your dreams. Think not about your frustrations,
> but about your unfulfilled potential. Concern
> yourself not with what you tried and failed in,
> but with what it is still possible for you to do.
> **—POPE JOHN XXIII**[28]

What's keeping you from achieving your dream? Is it where you live, the parents you had, the economy, the company you work for, God's destiny for you?

Dr. Peale said, "Through prayer you . . . make use of the great factor within yourself, the deep subconscious mind . . . [which Jesus called] the kingdom of God within you. . . . Positive

thinking is just another term for faith."[29] Are you releasing the
kingdom of God within you or blocking it with your sense of
being a doofus?

I believe life is what we believe it is. We create our own
reality around us every minute of the day. The thoughts
we dwell on are the ones most likely to come into fruition.

For many years I believed I would always have *just
enough*. And I always did. About three years ago I decided
that it was time to expect abundance, that I would have
more than enough so I could freely give to others.

I spent many years struggling just to survive. And as
ole Maslow famously posited, if we're constantly struggling
just to survive, it's much more difficult to give as much
attention to any other aspect of life.

The last three years of believing for abundance have
paid off. Just a year ago my wife and I were living back in
Nashville for a short spell after five years in Rwanda. We
had dreamed of moving to Mombasa and living the beautiful life of the Swahili Coast.

We had no real plan for getting here. We just believed
it would happen. We scrounged up about $5,000 and
decided to go for it. We spent $3,400 on airline tickets,
about $500 on supplies to take with us, and then left for a
month of consulting in Rwanda.

At the end of April 2011, we headed to Mombasa. I
had already purchased our tickets from Kigali to Mombasa
because I wanted to lock us in to taking the leap. I knew
if we got back to Rwanda, we'd be too tempted to jump
right back into a world we already knew and in which we
felt comfortable.

By then, we were down to $700, and we didn't know a soul in Mombasa. Neither of us had even been there before. On our first full day in Mombasa, an old man offered to change $100 of US currency for us. A few minutes later he was nowhere to be found.

I didn't even have the heart to tell Ilea. She was worried enough as it was. I just believed that we would get the money back somehow and that we were supposed to be here. I walked out from the little alley where the man had stolen our money and put a smile on my face, and we headed to the beach.

About two weeks later I got another consulting client. That gave us enough money to survive a few more months. About six weeks later I landed the biggest consulting job I've ever gotten, working for the largest coffee trader in Kenya.

I signed a three-month contract that paid us enough to move into the house we wanted on the beach, furnish it, and have plenty left over to make it a home, not just a house. Two months into my contract I got an extension contract for twelve more months with increasing pay during that time.

Although they fly me to Nairobi often, I still work from home most of the time. They gave me a car, and there are lots of other perks. But most important, I love my work, it pays me well, and I'm contributing daily to fostering ethical business practices in Kenya that provide hundreds of great jobs across the country.

This is what can happen when we start to change our perspectives, believe in ourselves, and shoot for the stars.

If You Can't Describe What You Want, Don't Say You Never Had a Chance

The people who complain the loudest about never having an opportunity in life are usually the ones who have no idea what they really want. They end up as what Zig Ziglar calls "wandering generalities."[30] They aren't happy where they are but can't tell you where they want to be.

And nothing is their fault. They are victims of the economy, their upbringing, their lack of education, the country they live in, or the evil company they work for. The real world puts them at a disadvantage. I know a guy who just got out of prison after ten years. He's now suing the prison because they did not adjust the temperature to his liking while he was incarcerated—definitely unfair. I just got a lengthy e-mail from a fifty-year-old man who says he has "never had any success in life" because of the way his parents control him.

And yes, any of us can find reasons for not attempting something spectacular—reasons for the mediocrity we have settled for.

Successful people, however, are not excuse makers. They take responsibility for their actions and the results they get. Where others see obstacles, frustration, discouragement, and despair, they see hope and opportunity. They approach every situation with the enthusiasm, confidence, and boldness that come only from having a clear plan of action and the anticipation of a positive outcome.

If you've never had a chance, an even break, or the right opportunity, check with the person in the mirror. He or she has the keys for the success you're looking for.

WE DO WHAT WE WANT

Most people want more money, more time, and better relationships. They want to lose more weight, work out more, finally go on that trip to Africa, or whatever the case may be.

But when it comes to putting in the work, things change. Most of us want the results of having a daily workout routine but fail to discipline ourselves to do it. We want to travel the world but not do the work that leads to the financial ability to do so.

For every excuse we have for not doing something, we can look back in history and find someone even more disadvantaged who did it anyway. Think of the Olympic athletes with prosthetic limbs, the Helen Kellers of the world, and so on. They wanted it, they believed, and they chose to make it happen, no matter what.

We lock ourselves into imaginary boundaries from which we do not stray. Civilizations have done this since the beginning of humanity. But no matter where you come from, the education you never obtained, the family you never had, or the circumstances you are in, you can choose to follow your dreams. Just stop doing what you've always done, and take steps in the direction you want to go.

From the way we treat people around us, to our careers, to our humanitarian endeavors, to our character, to our weight, we make a series of choices based on what is most important to us.

It's a lot easier to just say, "That's impossible," or "I don't have enough money/education/time." But I believe we all ultimately do exactly what we want to do; it's just a matter of how badly we want it. And I don't believe it's any more complicated than that.

I Can Predict Your Future

No, I'm not a fortune-teller or prophet. I can't see into your mind, and I don't need to know your history, your degrees, or your family. All I need to do is spend a day with you, listen to what you say, and watch what you do. Your words and your actions will tell me exactly where you are going to be five years from now.

One of our 48 Days coaches had a conversation with an old friend who predicted what his day would hold.[31] As they parted ways he said, "I'd better go see who won't hire me today." What do you think he will experience in the workplace? His expectations that we are in a recession, everyone is laying off workers, and no companies are hiring will be confirmed by the words he is speaking in advance.

I ran into a guy in Best Buy who said he had downloaded my 48 Low-Cost Business Ideas.[32] Then he added, "But I'm a technology guy, so none of those would work for me." The list linked to another one thousand ideas, but he was absolutely right. None of those would've worked for him because his expectations set the stage for his reality.

The Bible is clear about the power of our words. Check this out from *The Message*: "It only takes a spark, remember, to set off a forest fire. A careless or wrongly placed word out of your mouth can do that. By our speech we can ruin the world, turn harmony to chaos, throw mud on a reputation, send the whole world up in smoke and go up in smoke with it, smoke right from the pit of hell" (James 3:5–6).

Your life five years from now will not be determined by the

economy, the political climate, luck, your education, the lottery, or your astrological sign.

What kind of future are your words and actions creating?

I'm Good but Not Great

There is a PBS special on the music of David Foster.[33]As the host asked him about his early years in music, one response jumped out at me. David said he loved music as a child, and his parents allowed him to take lessons in classical music. David added that he was good but not great. He went on to explain that if he had been a better musician, he likely would have ended up as an anonymous face in some orchestra. Not being great forced him to look for other ways to be involved in music. So he writes and produces for other musicians. It has been said that Foster's songs have made many famous singers into superstars. Many of his songs have become well known through the voices of Celine Dion, Barbra Streisand, Andrea Bocelli, Josh Groban, the late Whitney Houston, Madonna, Michael Bublé, and Boz Scaggs. And his own fame and fortune have far surpassed what he could have possibly hoped for as a great musician.

In his book *The Millionaire Mind*, author Thomas Stanley examines the common characteristics of people who have ended up extremely wealthy. Their average GPA is 2.7.[34] Why isn't it that all 4.0 students become wildly successful? Maybe their greatness came too easily, and they missed the benefits of the struggle.

If greatness has not come easily for you, have you given up the pursuit and settled for mediocrity? Or have you looked for alternative approaches for success anyway?

Maybe greatness that comes too easily is itself an obstacle. We've all seen athletes, musicians, writers, and speakers who were so naturally great that they never had to exercise the discipline to survive the hard times—and quickly faded into oblivion.

Maybe not being great is your biggest hidden asset. What could you do to stand out, to be remarkable in your field of interest, even if you will never be the greatest in the traditional way?

EVERYTHING IS GOOD FOR YOU

People so often become paralyzed by their failures. I don't view such instances, though, as failures at all; they are necessary steps to success. It's not in the moments of abundance or joy that our character is strengthened. It's in the moments when we overcome obstacles and recover from perceived failures that our souls are freed and our true selves are revealed.

When I first went to Rwanda, I was dead set on petitioning the government for better policies on women's rights and letting the public know we would not settle for anything less than complete equality. But I was inexperienced and naive and soon learned that this sort of behavior only brought more scrutiny and oppression to the women I was there to serve. It put them in the crosshairs.

Only after four years of turmoil, incarceration, interrogation, public persecution, and even being framed for defamation did I learn how to truly serve the women of Rwanda. I never could have learned these lessons in a book or through a conference. I had to experience it. There was a path I was destined to travel. Had I refrained from my initial urge to fight the system, I never would have stumbled into the knowledge I have now. I had to learn these things.

I am of the belief that everything that happens to us

is either good or a path to achieving something good through the lessons learned. It's our choice. We can be paralyzed or defeated from these instances, or we can choose to dissect them, analyze them, and create a new system or practice that reflects the lessons learned.

I will never approach a human rights issue the way I did before. I learned a lesson. It was necessary, and I am grateful for that experience.

> Expose yourself to your deepest fear; after that, fear has no power, and the fear of freedom shrinks and vanishes. You are free.
> —JIM MORRISON[35]

I Just Don't Fit In

Joanne and I have a tradition of watching the 1994 movie *Little Women* while we put up our Christmas decorations. Jo (Winona Ryder), the main character, is a creative, energetic young woman who finds it difficult to do the normal things in that town and culture. Fortunately she has an insightful and understanding mother (Susan Sarandon).

After having just rejected a marriage proposal from her longtime boyfriend, Jo verbalizes her exasperation with herself: "There is something wrong with me. I'll never fit in anywhere." Her mother gently replies, "You have so many extraordinary gifts. How could you expect to lead an ordinary life?"

I love those words of wisdom. What a blessing to have a mother with that kind of insight, a mother who validates her daughter's uniqueness rather than squashes it.

Do you have someone in your life who encourages your unique gifts? Or are you still experiencing pressure to do what is practical and realistic? Do you find it difficult to fit in? If so, maybe you just need to stop expecting to lead an ordinary life.

I grew up on a farm in Ohio, just outside a little town that to this day does not have a traffic light. The expectation was that I would do the normal thing: marry a local girl and continue farming. But I could see more than milking cows and throwing hay bales. As a little boy I envisioned being other places and doing work that rewarded thinking and writing rather than just raw physical effort. Fortunately I found books that supported my dreams and visions, and I found a way not to lead an ordinary life.

In the movie, Jo's mother continued, "Go embrace your liberty and see what wonderful things come of it." Maybe your destiny is not to accept an ordinary life, with ordinary success, income, and sense of fulfillment. Perhaps your path is to explore, create, embrace, and follow the road less traveled and live a truly extraordinary life.

Do you find it difficult to fit in?

Can you identify your extraordinary gifts that make it challenging to be normal?

Find ways to embrace the things that make you unique and you'll unlock the ways you can make a difference in the world.

> If one advances confidently in the direction
> of his dreams, and endeavors to live the life
> which he had imagined, he will meet with a
> success unexpected in common hours.
> **—HENRY DAVID THOREAU**[36]

The Fire of Genius Was Extinguished

People ask me, "Do I really think each person is unique? And should each person's work reflect that uniqueness?" Yes and yes. History has shown repeatedly that whenever we remove the individuality of people, the culture ultimately fails.

Sir Edward Gibbon, English historian and member of Parliament, wrote *The History of the Decline and Fall of the Roman Empire*. He outlined how "the uniform government of the Romans introduced a slow and secret poison into the vitals of the empire. The minds of men were gradually reduced to the same level, the fire of genius was extinguished."[37]

Ouch—the fire of genius was extinguished.

As far back as 1776, Adam Smith saw the dangers of removing the uniqueness of each person's work. In his highly influential *The Wealth of Nations*, he wrote that a person who spends his life performing the same repetitive tasks "generally becomes as stupid and ignorant as it is possible for a human creature to become."[38] Wow! Now that's not a pretty picture.

Since 1925 we have moved toward jobs that remove human uniqueness and specialized talent. Assembly lines, cubicles, tenure, and vested retirement plans have brought us inter- changeable parts—and interchangeable workers. The lack of individuality and uniqueness in many of our jobs today is disabling the human spirit and reducing the minds of men to the same level.

The demise of big corporations and the loss of a secure job may be painful—and it also may be just the wake-up call needed to redeem the fire of your genius.

Does your work embrace your genius? Could you describe work that does?

How easy would it be to replace you in your current position?

Are you in a transition—an opportunity to wake up your genius?

The more you understand yourself, the more prepared you are to make a difference in your family, your work, your community, your country, and the world.

For decades aid workers, developers, and governments have been struggling to get Africa up to speed with China, the United States, and other mass producers. They've ignorantly tried to strip the uniqueness out of the culture and replace it with a mass mentality. Consequently, Africa has lost a bit of its soul and entered a game in which it will never succeed.

Africa has one of the most pure and diverse cultures in the world. There is so much uniqueness and robust culture here. We don't need to strip that out and make way for assembly lines. We need to channel it into a sustainable system for income generation.

Imagine if great artists like Jackson Pollock, Wolfgang Amadeus Mozart, Tom Waits, Vincent van Gogh, and others had extinguished their genius because of pressure from the status-quo-governed public. Think of the beauty our society would have lost.

We need to foster the individual uniqueness of Africa's true art and value it accordingly. People want quality, uniqueness, innovation, and in many respects, exclusivity. When everything is the same, the value plummets. When you see something unique, you'll pay a bit more for that individuality.

Rather than conform to the status quo and extinguish the fire of genius, we should develop an atmosphere that rewards that mentality both financially and socially.

CHAPTER TWO

Where Do I Find Security?

I met with a young man who was considering leaving his current job. While he enjoys the freedom he has, he doesn't feel he has much security. The organization he's working for can't give him guaranteed raises, 401(k) benefits, and a car allowance. He'd prefer to be in an organization where he still has lots of freedom but where there is more security.

I tried to gently show him that those two concepts are totally opposed. If you want ultimate freedom to get up when you want to get up, decide what you're going to do today, and have no ceiling on your income possibilities; then obviously you will have to work for yourself. As soon as you expect someone else to give you security, you begin to give up your freedom. The ultimate example would be inmates in maximum-security prisons. They have the most security and the least freedom.

Baby boomers expected to graduate, find a job with the right company (security), work thirty-five years, get that proverbial gold watch, and enjoy the remaining retirement years. They thought wisdom would pave the way to success. Today's younger generations, however, rely on passion as the guiding principle for their versions of success. The implosion of major companies, such as Enron, WorldCom, AIG, Bear Stearns, Countrywide, Merrill Lynch, Borders, Hollywood Video, and Tower Records, has done little to reduce the cynicism of Generations X and Y. While mom and dad talked about consistency, loyalty, and commitment, the children saw unpredictability, disloyalty, and abuse of power from the very institutions being held out as worthy models.

For many, the so-called American Dream is lost forever. Now the younger generations are rebuilding the ideals supporting the original American Dream. This is the beginning of the "new world" in many respects. It's not that the dream is being discarded—it simply means it looks different. For example, in his "We Can All Live in Wonderland" blog post, Jared wrote, "I live in a world full of dreams, faith, and whimsy where anything is possible if you believe. Relationships always trump trivial things like time, money, and comfort. Each step of life is raw and deliberate. I believe loyalty, vulnerability, and honesty to be among the most imperative of characteristics. And I believe there is purpose to everything."[1]

Popular music, movies, and social networks reveal the disdain for established traditions and expectations. Groups like Rage Against the Machine[2] and Coldplay[3] speak out, calling fans to defy the corporate machine, treat others fairly, and do something worthwhile. "Seize the day," "leave a legacy," and "do something that matters" are no longer trite clichés—rather, they are the driving forces of Generations X and Y. Yes, the twenty-somethings lag behind previous generations in some of the traditional criteria for adulthood—finishing school, leaving home, getting married, having children, buying a first house, and attaining financial independence. Frequently there are accusations that those in their twenties are just not acting like adults. But is acting like the baby boomers the accurate model of adulthood, or are we simply seeing a new definition of growing up? Baby boomers valued the concept of growing up because it implied that children would go from being irresponsible to responsible. But their idea of responsibility included being less spontaneous and having a mortgage, a 401(k), and a stock portfolio. For many in the next generations, that is irrelevant to what they would consider success. They may see those identifiers as the opposite of real success—tying one down to a life of predictability and smothering vibrant living. They see the traditional life as settling for mediocrity and taking the path of least resistance. There is no attraction to being normal or ordinary. In fact, that's a terrifying prospect.

The new generations want to change the world. Nothing is more frightening than the prospect of mediocrity. Yes, they may appear narcissistic—self-centered rather than other-focused. But they are looking for redemption, for a cause that validates their very existence. They want family and a strong sense of community, but they may accomplish that desire through a social network where there is never any physical contact or presence. Yes, they want to make a sustainable impact on the world, but they resist the methods of traditional business. Yes, they want to be educated, but they don't have the time or patience to sit in a classroom chair for four years. They know that a well-rounded knowledge of culture, business, and strategies is needed, but they regard spending four years out of the game and being saddled with thousands of dollars in student loan debt as limits on the immediate options for making a difference.[4] More and more, college-age adults are realizing the impact of internships and volunteering. They understand that they can learn through actual application much more quickly than studying hours of theory in a classroom completely detached from reality. They confidently believe that passion, determination, talent, self-discipline, and faith will override the benefits of slower and more historical methods for creating change. Like Henry David Thoreau, they want to "live deep and suck out all the marrow of life," and when they come to die, they do not want to "discover that [they] had not lived."[5]

So do you want the passion of youth or the wisdom that comes with age? Perhaps a better question is: Do you have to make that choice? Is it possible to maintain the passion of youth into old age and to attain the wisdom commonly associated with maturity at an early age? As we continue through these chapters you will find that both are critical at any age. And you can expect to have both no matter where you are in your life's journey. Nothing is sadder than a young person with no passion. And few things are more pathetic than an older person without wisdom. Perhaps the biggest tragedy is seeing the thousands of baby boomers flocking to retirement centers with neither passion nor wisdom—looking back on a life with dreams unfulfilled and looking forward to the drab existence of meaningless days leading to ultimate death.

> Conformity is the jailer of freedom,
> and the enemy of growth.
> —JOHN F. KENNEDY[6]

Security or Freedom—You Can't Have Both

As soon as you line up where they expect you to be at a certain time in the morning, you've given up some of your freedom.

As soon as you demand a guaranteed income, you've given up the open-ended income possibilities.

As soon as you negotiate for a paid vacation, you've given up the freedom to choose when and how long you vacation.

I know salespeople who are guaranteed $10 an hour and would scream if that guarantee were taken away. And they consistently make $400 a week. The salespeople I know who make $300,000 a year have no guarantee. They just do what they do well and are paid according to the results they produce. The people I see at the beach two months out of the year, who travel around the world at will, who work late at night and then sleep till noon the next day, or who take sixty days to write a bestseller—these people have no 401(k) plan, no provided medical insurance, no company car, no time clock, and no paid coffee breaks. They just have freedom and the absence of ceilings in any area of chosen success.

Only the insecure strive for security.

—WAYNE DYER[7]

This is not a right-or-wrong issue. It's just a matter of choice.

The more security you desire, the less freedom you will have. The more freedom you want, the less security you will have. You get to choose.

It has been said that security is one's ability to produce. Security no longer comes from longevity, seniority, or a retirement package. It will not likely come from a bailout plan or Social Security. So how can we find—or create—our own security? The new model requires having transferable skills and understanding the power of community.

Our son, Francois, is Rwandan, and he had never left the country until December 12, 2011. This is his first time in

Kenya, a country vastly different from his homeland in terms of politics and culture.

During the first week, he noted that Kenya is quite dirty, or at least it is here in Mombasa. There is trash everywhere, and little dumps have sprung up alongside the road. The government doesn't have any mechanism for waste management, so people just throw the trash on the ground. With no alternative, it's hard to blame them.

However, Francois also wisely noted, "But there is freedom." This is something he has not experienced on this level in Rwanda. Yes, there is a lot of trash on the ground, it is more dangerous, and there is less order, but there is freedom in Kenya. You can create a business easily, say what you want, go where you want, think freely, innovate, be creative, and indulge in many other aspects of a free nation.

With freedom comes a level of insecurity and risk. You can choose safety, security, and order, or you can choose freedom, creativity, and mystery. I will always choose the latter because I believe the risk of getting wounded along the way is less than the risk of never having lived at all. I also believe that the wounds I collect along the way represent the refining I need to become the man I was created to be.

Every human has four endowments—self-awareness, conscience, independent will and creative imagination. These give us the ultimate human freedom. . . . The power to choose, to respond, to change.

—STEPHEN COVEY[8]

I'd Try Freedom, but I Don't Have Any Money

The most common complaint I hear today is, "Dan, I'd do something on my own, but I don't have any money." Fortunately many of the best ideas do not require buildings, leases, employees, or inventory. And many can be started with very little, if any, capital.

Here are recent examples:

- A hunter got an option on four hundred isolated acres, then sold forty hunting licenses for $5,000 each. He then completed the purchase free and clear and pocketed approximately $50,000.
- An artifacts dealer arranged an exhibit for some rare Dead Sea Scroll pieces. Thirty thousand people came through a minimally promoted showing in a small town. Now he is opening in a major city, anticipating fifty thousand viewers at $19 each. You do the math.
- A computer guy discovered the internal battery on his Apple computer needed to be replaced at a cost of about $125. He researched and found a small tool at Sears for $3 and the batteries in bulk for $2 each. With these and a one-page explanation he created a repair kit for this common problem. In a sixty-day period he sold seven hundred kits at $24.95 each.
- An artist received a comment that her paintings were peaceful. This comment triggered a thought that people going to dentists' offices needed a peaceful surrounding. She has been immensely successful by going to dentists' conventions—likely the only artist there—and selling her paintings to dentists.
- A high school student went to garage sales with his mother to buy Disney items. He then placed them

on eBay, netting approximately $3,000 monthly in anticipation of beginning college. Kinda beats the $8 hourly job at McDonald's.

- Another client wanted to be in the antique business but had no money. He negotiated a ninety-day lease option on a warehouse, dividing it into seventy-two spaces for an antique mall. In a sixty-day period he rented seventy spaces, collecting first and last months' rent. With this $7,000 he completed the lease, did minimal renovations, and opened for business. His rent is $1,500, and he is collecting $3,500. In addition, he has two spaces for his own merchandise and receives a 10 percent commission on everyone's sales.

- One of our 48 Days coaches wanted to write a book. He got eleven other coaches to submit a chapter. Then he had them pay $3,500 each to get five hundred copies for themselves (a 50 percent discount off retail). He printed the books showing himself as the lead author, put a clean $30,000 in his pocket, and continues to have the contributing authors purchase books from him.

What's your idea? Keep in mind, ideas alone don't put any money in your pocket. You must *act*!

Finding Your Pot of Gold

Gold was discovered in California in the spring of 1848. By May 1848 reports were flying that there was more gold than all the people in California could take out in fifty years. Twenty-eight-year-old Samuel Brannan opened a small supply store at John Sutter's Fort, right in the heart of the gold rush. Brannan purchased a little vial of gold and traveled the hundred miles back to San Francisco. As he stepped off the train, he swung his hat, waved the bottle, and shouted, "Gold! Gold! Gold!" By the middle of June, three-quarters of the male population had left town for the gold mines near Sutter's Fort.

Here's a pretty interesting side note: Brannan never looked for gold, but selling shovels, picks, and supplies to the wide-eyed miners made him California's first millionaire. His store was selling as much as $5,000 a day (about $140,000 in 2012 dollars) in goods to the miners.[9]

Did all the miners find their pots of gold? Not a chance. Most of them wasted time and meager resources only to return to their original homes, poor and discouraged.

So where are you looking for income opportunities? In the last ten years, thousands of people jumped on the computer bandwagon, believing that programming, web design, and software development were the only real sources of wealth. As you know, not everyone going in this direction has become wealthy. But are there associated opportunities with this area of focus? Absolutely!

In the last ten years the number of massage therapists has quadrupled. (Our massage therapist comes to our house every Friday afternoon.) People who work on computers all day are prime candidates for massage.

I have a friend here in Nashville who produced a novelty red panic button that fits over any key on your computer keyboard.[10] She has now sold more than 100,000 at $1.50 each. A convent even ordered ten panic buttons.

I have talented young musician friends who are not trying to be the next Alan Jackson but are generating significant income selling guitar straps,[11] personalized drum sticks,[12] and a book on how to make it in the music industry.[13]

Is it possible that in your own search for gold you are over-looking the opportunity to become a millionaire by selling picks and shovels to the miners?

Employee vs. Free Agent

In professional football or baseball, a free agent is a player whose contract with a team has expired and who is thus eligible to sign with another club or franchise.

In today's workplace most people are, in fact, free agents.[14] They have no contract, and they are free to negotiate with a new "team" if they choose. Yet many people just stay because they continue to get a paycheck—without even looking around to see if they could get a better offer.

Who are free agent workers? Free agents don't expect (or want) a lifetime career with a single employer. They have taken responsibility for charting and preparing their own professional futures.

Changing jobs is commonplace. Free agent workers think of themselves as having talent to sell, and they shop it around for the best offer.

We are seeing many challenges to the traditional *employee* work model. Companies resist guaranteeing pay for time as opposed to results. In many ways this is a healthy correction of an unrealistic business model. Thus we are seeing an explosion of consultants, contingency workers, independent contractors, temps, entrepreneurs, electronic immigrants, and so on.

A person between ages eighteen and forty-four will have an average of 10.8 different jobs.[15] We can no longer be identified by *who we work for.*

To shift from employee to free agent, you must

- clarify your most marketable skills;
- describe yourself in terms of the kind of work you do, not who you work for;
- recognize you may have one or several "customers"; and
- be confident you can move up in your career even while moving from company to company.

If the idea of being a free agent is appealing, check out the growing community at this site: 48Days.net. These are people just like you who are linking arms, sharing ideas and resources, and shaping their ideas into productive, meaningful, and profitable work.

Which Player Are You?

Picture this scenario. A businessman has purchased coffee samples from fifty local farmers. The next morning he loads up the samples in his cart behind his faithful donkey. He dangles a carrot in front of the donkey's nose. The businessman is already thinking about all the orders he's going to get from these delectable samples. The donkey has no idea where they're going or why—he doesn't even like coffee; he's simply following the carrot just in front of his nose. At the end of the day, the donkey gets the carrot and looks forward to another task tomorrow, with another carrot as the reward. The businessman has the potential of something really big. If he gets even a few orders, he will leverage his skill and knowledge dramatically.

If you're working nine to five, you know your role in this little story. Lots of you have been telling us you want to be the guy in the cart, not the donkey.

Poor people trade their time for money—or carrots. The problem is that time is limited; there is always a ceiling on your possible income. If you're in the coffee business and you get an order for an additional fifty thousand bags, you call your suppliers, deliver that quantity, and count your profits. If you're working by the hour and your boss says he has an opportunity for you to work an extra fifty thousand hours, what can you do? If you're being paid twenty dollars an hour, that's a cool $1 million, but you can't deliver. Even at eighty hours a week, it would take you the next twelve years to cash in. How frustrating is that?

WHEN GREATNESS IS EXPECTED

The developed world has always viewed Africa as being worthy only of endless laborers and cheap trinkets. This pervasive belief has raised up nations of people convinced that their only value is that of a donkey. They work for a carrot, and it's over. Repeat. In many respects, this mentality has robbed Africa of some of its soul and much of its art.

The aid world talks incessantly about "sustainability" in Africa, especially in reference to setting up businesses. Isn't that the least we would expect from a business in the West? If I operated a business in Nashville, Tennessee, it's unlikely I'd consider myself a success if I merely kept the doors open year after year. Yet this seems to be the most we expect of Africa.

I feel that this is yet another great injustice we have imposed on Africa.

Why don't we expect greatness? And what might

happen if we did? John Steinbeck once said, "It is the nature of men to rise to greatness if greatness is expected of them."[16] Is it possible that a people group might rise to greatness if it was continually expected of them?

If we desire to empower Africa to pull itself out of poverty and achieve economic independence from aid agencies and government, we must set the bar higher. We cannot settle for sustainable businesses; they must be sustainable at the very least with the ultimate goal of profitability.

If we expect mediocrity, everyone involved is set up for failure and disappointment. Might we be contributing to the problem with these low expectations? We've got to strive for better. There are many components that will contribute to Africa's success, but I believe this is integral to sending them on the right trajectory.

> Americans are so enamored of equality
> that they would rather be equal in
> slavery than unequal in freedom.
> **—ALEXIS DE TOCQUEVILLE**[17]

Do You Really Want That Free Lunch?

Years ago in Monterey, California, a crisis arose. Monterey had become a paradise for pelicans. After cleaning their fish, the local fishermen threw all the excess waste to the pelicans. The birds soon became fat and lazy. Baby pelicans grew up dependent on the handouts, not knowing how to catch their next meal.

Eventually a new market was found that could use the waste

products commercially. The pelicans no longer had a free meal. Yet the pelicans made no effort to fish for themselves. Generations had been trained to just wait and wait for the free handouts, but they never came. The birds were angry and resentful about the unexpected changes. Many starved to death. They seemed to have forgotten how to fish for themselves.

Are there possibly examples of human pelicans?

1. *Unemployment.* After the depths of the Great Depression, unemployment benefits were established in 1935 to assist unemployed people.[18] The state and federal funds were to provide five to fifteen dollars per week and would be paid for not more than sixteen weeks. Today people are demanding that unemployment benefits be extended beyond ninety-nine weeks. And yet we know that the biggest predictor of how long someone will be unemployed is how long that person has access to unemployment benefits.

2. *Welfare.* Our welfare system was established to help those few people who struggle most. Today we have entire families into the third and fourth generations who have no expectation of income other than government welfare. If we assume generosity generates gratitude, then we would expect these people to be the most grateful and patriotic of all segments of our society. What we see is that these communities are hot spots of anger, hostility, resentment, and violence.

3. *Foreign aid.* In an op-ed piece in the *Wall Street Journal,* Dambisa Moyo writes that "charity-based aid" cannot provide long-term sustainable

development for Africa. She says the sixty trillion dollars of this aid that's been given in the past sixty years is not working, evident from the fact that the number of Africans who live on less than one dollar a day has doubled in the last twenty years. Anger and resentment against the United States are growing. We have destroyed the profitability of local farmers, gardeners, clothing makers, and shoe sellers. Moyo says cutting off the flow of foreign aid would be "far more beneficial."[19]

When does helping start hurting? If we want those pelicans to develop their natural talent for fishing, what is the most helpful thing we can do?

> Money won't create success, the
> freedom to make it will.
> **—NELSON MANDELA**[20]

THE INDUSTRY OF AID:
WHY IS AFRICA A CHARITY CASE?

Africa is the second-largest continent, bursting with more natural resources than any other, yet still behind much of the rest of the world in terms of economic development, peace, and health.

Why? There is no simple answer, but there are some consistently predominant contributors.

Precolonization, Africa was peaceful and self-reliant. Colonials moved in, did their usual raping and pillaging of the people and land, and continue to do these things today. They created systems for oppression, demoralization, and divisionism, exemplified in catastrophes like the Rwandan genocide.

Then came the missionaries and humanitarians, determined to save the helpless Africans and make them "civilized." Decades later, much of this process has evolved into yet another oppressive and controlling system, quite contrary to the original mission, yet certainly endemic of their behavior.

There is a pervasive belief that Africa is inferior, unable to develop and prosper on its own. Africa is overflowing with aid agencies and NGOs (nongovernmental organizations) that rely on its ongoing struggle. The maladies found in the nations of Africa provide these groups with jobs and income. They depend on Africa's plight. This is a broken system.

The colonialists see Africa as a playground of free resources and endless slave labor. Aid agencies treat Africa as a charity case, creating systems that ensure their services are always needed.

Aid is an industry, generating billions of dollars per year for these institutions. Continents like Africa have become their cash cow. And aid is now a major cog in our world economy.

So why can't we treat Africa as our greatest asset, a destination for business? Why aren't those billions of dollars in aid money used to create businesses instead of institutions that foster dependency on donors (for aid workers and recipients alike)?

Why is Africa recognized as the world's largest charity case?

Developing nations are not often recognized for excellence. However, this has little to do with the level of talent and determination found in these areas. There are thousands of extraordinary artisans and competent entrepreneurs yet to have the opportunity to present their designs and products to the international market.

Decades of focus on the negative aspects of these nations have created a pervasive image of inferiority. But we know firsthand about the tremendous wealth of talent found there. As long as we treat these nations as charity cases, we will continue to limit their capabilities and (negatively) influence their level of output.

I must note that during my five years living in East Africa, I have experienced countless NGOs and aid agencies that are saving lives and having a positive impact on society. My comments here reflect the scores of others I've witnessed that are regularly contributing to Africa's demise, many of them knowingly.

May we think of freedom, not as the right to do as we
please but as the opportunity to do what is right.
—PETER MARSHALL JR.[21]

Be Undeniably Good

So how do you put yourself in a position to act on your passion and wisdom? How do you know you are ready to step out and do something meaningful to yourself and others? While there are many aspects of what it takes to be successful, here is one quick tip from actor and comedian Steve Martin:

> Be undeniably good. When people ask me how do you make it in show business or whatever, what I always tell them and nobody ever takes note of it 'cause it's not the answer they wanted to hear—what they want to hear is here's how you get an agent, here's how you write a script, here's how you do this—but I always say, "Be so good they can't ignore you." If somebody's thinking, "How can I be really good?" people are going to come to you. It's much easier doing it that way than going to cocktail parties.[22]

I love this principle of just being so good at something that people can't ignore you. Steve Martin always used the banjo as a prop for his comedy routines and over time became really, really good at playing it.

Have you identified the area in which you are undeniably good?

> If a man is called to be a street sweeper, he should sweep streets even as Michelangelo painted or Beethoven composed music or Shakespeare wrote poetry. He should sweep streets so well that all the hosts of heaven and earth will pause to say: Here lived a great street sweeper who did his job well.
> **—DR. MARTIN LUTHER KING JR.[23]**

Talent Is Never Enough

Whoa! Didn't I just say become so good that you can't be ignored? Yes, but that's not the only issue in sustaining success. In *48 Days to the Work You Love*, I stress the importance of making deposits of success in seven areas of life:[24]

1. financial
2. social
3. personal development
4. physical
5. spiritual
6. family
7. career

Only by being successful in each of these areas do we attain success that is worth having.

I have been dumbfounded recently when I have run into several longtime acquaintances who are down on their luck. These guys were used to going first class all the way—restaurants, cars, private flights, yachts, and houses. One told me he has been selling his clothes on eBay to pay the apartment rent, parking the car because gas is too expensive, and eating at McDonald's.

My assumption has always been that if someone has never gotten off the ground, he may not know how, but that once someone is up, he can bounce back again quickly even if a real estate swing or bad investment strategy caught him unprepared. Why would a guy like that get trapped in a down position and seem to stay there?

I began researching, asking, and studying to see if there were any common factors. I pulled a 2007 John Maxwell book, *Talent Is Never Enough*, off my shelf and reread it. John says that people's "talent allows them to stand out, but their wrong choices make them sit down."[25] I was reminded how character, integrity, relationships, and responsibility are the pillars that allow talent to shine. Without those pillars the shining talent is very vulnerable.

I grieve for my friends who are down, and I am harshly reminded of the importance of not leaning too strongly on talent in my life. Unless I'm making deposits of success in character, integrity, and relationships, I could find myself holding a tin cup full of pencils.

How much of a factor has talent been to your success?

Are there other areas where you need to make more deposits of success?

Disclaimer: Please, please don't assume I'm implying that everyone who is down is lacking in character and integrity. There are many reasons for a person's position at any given time. I've just been researching to find ways to be more helpful as a friend.

> Freedom makes a huge requirement of every
> human being. With freedom comes responsibility.
> For the person who is unwilling to grow up,
> the person who does not want to carry his
> own weight, this is a frightening prospect.
> **—ELEANOR ROOSEVELT**[26]

What is more important to you: freedom or security? Do you see why you may need to redefine what those terms mean? Remember this line from the old Janis Joplin song "Me and Bobby McGee": "Freedom's just another word for nothing left to lose"? Freedom with no balance of responsibility is not really freedom; that can trap us into subservience to something undesirable. Yeah, feeling good may be easy, but if feeling good comes from using drugs, having illicit sex, or taking advantage of others, then it's not really freedom but another enslavement to something undesirable.

Choose freedom in a way that releases your strongest talents, your personality traits, and your values, dreams, and passions.

> Those who deny freedom to others
> deserve it not for themselves.
>
> **—ABRAHAM LINCOLN**[27]

CHAPTER THREE

I Owe $133,000 and Can't Find a Job

"Chuck" and "Susan" bounded into my office. At twenty-seven and twenty-nine years old, respectively, they looked the part of the perfect American couple. Having completed their master's degrees in the previous month, they were excited and optimistic about the opportunities awaiting them. Chuck had his brand-new diploma showing his MA in Bible history while Susan displayed her MS in social work. Yes, they had that nagging little issue of $133,000 in student loan debt, but the school they attended had continuously encouraged them to ignore any concerns about that. They were assured that the advanced degrees they were pursuing would open doors to plenty of jobs.

I was more than a little concerned, however. While personable, attractive, and enthusiastic, Chuck and Susan had degrees that did not assure them lucrative first positions. After spending time with this lovely young couple, I told Chuck I could see him in perhaps a $28,000-a-year first job. He was mortified and assured me very quickly that he would not con-sider anything less than $80,000. With years of career coaching behind me, I attempted to help him frame his skill set and identify how he could add value to a company. With his degree focus he could be a candidate for a teaching opportunity or per-haps a staff position with a church. But he assured me he was not interested in either possibility and had more of a corporate executive position in mind. Chuck wrote out a description of a position where "I would call the shots. I would be allowed and trusted to identify needs, solve problems, produce results, and make decisions." With a strong faith this couple also believed that God would providentially guide them to the positions they imagined.

As we continued to work through this challenging pro-cess, I suggested that his appealing personal skills could be best used in a sales position or perhaps an entrepreneurial venture. But Chuck was reluctant to be paid only for results. Surely he deserved guaranteed executive compensation for the years he had invested in schooling. Susan shared his hope that with her degree she would receive offers in the $70,000 to $80,000 range. We modified resumes to strengthen marketable skills while I gently coached them through the process of targeting compa-nies, getting interviews, and negotiating salaries.

You can perhaps guess the next chapter in this common story. With high hopes confronted by real-world reality, Chuck and Susan quickly became disheartened. Three months into the job search, Chuck wrote, "I have become a little discouraged and am exploring other possibilities. We have a lot of loans coming up and I don't feel like I am worth much to anyone. I feel like I have exhausted everything of interest and this has taken us back to the drawing board. . . . I want to start providing and to feel like a real man."

Their responses to my inquiries became less frequent as the discouragement mounted. Twenty-two months after our first meeting I received an angry e-mail: "We could have used the money we spent with you to move out of this rat-hole we live in. Now we are stuck!" They continued with an angry diatribe against the university that had encouraged them to go deeply in debt for earning "meaningless degrees," against corporate America for not recognizing their talent, and against God for letting them down so completely. I discovered they were living in government housing (welfare), were in default on their student loans, and had no jobs of any kind.

Obviously several issues emerge from this situation: false promises from a faith-based university, spiritual immaturity in expecting God to magically open doors, and unrealistic expectations for the real world of work.

> I think everyone should go to college and
> get a degree, and then spend six months as
> a bartender and six months as a cab driver.
> Then they would really be educated.
> **—AL MCGUIRE**[1]

The typical college student graduates with an overwhelming amount of student loan debt and yet struggles to find a job that allows for meager living expenses in addition to repayment of that debt. The myth of guaranteed success with a college degree has been exposed. Fortunately we are presented with opportunities every day to learn and improve ourselves outside traditional degree programs. And that improvement opens the door to new work, career, and business applications.

Learn and Grow Rich

I recently told someone that I think I'll throw up if I hear one more story about a young person having $100,000 in student loan debt but being unable to find a job. How can we continue perpetuating this myth that getting a college degree is the magic ticket to fame and fortune? Have we totally confused what real education is in this race for a piece of paper that guarantees little?

Before you jump to the conclusion that I am one of those radicals who denigrates college or that I dropped out and am bitter about never actually getting a degree, read on.

Later in this chapter I'm going to give you Ten Steps to Education and Becoming Rich. Just let me rant a little before we get to that part.

> I cannot teach anybody anything; I
> can only make them think.
> **—SOCRATES**[2]

Yes, we need education. But that occurs in many, many ways. When my son Kevin was racing bicycles in Europe as an eighteen-year-old, people asked me if I was concerned that he wasn't in college. My reply was that right then he was too busy getting an education to stop and go to college. Goodness me. Do you think perhaps that traveling internationally would be adding knowledge, information, and education that would surpass sitting in a classroom and regurgitating textbook facts?

College does not have a lock on education. The dictionary defines *education* as "the act or process of imparting or acquiring general knowledge, developing the powers of reasoning and judgment, and generally of preparing oneself or others intellectually for mature life." Education in the broadest sense is any experience or accumulation of knowledge that has a formative effect on the mind, spirit, character, or physical ability of an individual. The English word *education* is derived from the Latin *educere*, which means to "bring up," "bring out," or "bring forth what is within."[3] I'm confident you can identify many things that would accomplish those results. And education certainly should not end with the completion of any academic program.

Continual learning is the key to continual living. If you stop learning, you have effectively stopped living. Make this year the year to get the education you always wanted. Yes, in one year you can learn more valuable information than is often received in four or more years of college. My list of ten steps to becoming rich follows later in this chapter, and you can do all the steps in one year and for very little cost.

I have always enjoyed learning. But my education has come in a constant stream, sometimes added to by being in a classroom but mostly by taking advantage of the multitude of learning and enriching opportunities offered all around us.

> Formal education will make you a living.
> Self-education will make you a fortune.
>
> **—JIM ROHN[4]**

I was born into a conservative, rural Ohio family. With no radio or TV in the house, I found my information in books and became an avid reader. Torn between the need to provide for our family and the desire to embrace his spiritual calling, my father worked both as a farmer and as a pastor in the little local

Mennonite church. His double life instilled in me the idea that work was just a necessary evil and learning related only to the basics required for the farming chores. Working hard and being responsible left little time for anything playful or pleasurable. Frankly, anything that provided enjoyment was suspected of being self-serving, which further reinforced the idea that there was no merit in pure learning. Amusement parks, fancy cars, TV viewing, ball games, and "higher education" were examples of useless and dangerous activities that would likely pull a person away from what was eternally important. Exhausting farm work was a matter of survival; *education or work that you enjoyed demonstrated egotistical selfishness.*

Despite the limitations on the things I could do or the places I could go, nothing could stop my mind from wandering. As I was working out in the fields, I was also imagining a world I had never seen.

Somehow in that restricted world, when I was about twelve years old, I was able to get a copy of the little 33 1/3 record by Earl Nightingale titled *The Strangest Secret.* On it I heard this gravelly voiced man say that I could be everything I wanted to be by simply changing my thinking. He talked about six words that could dramatically affect the results of my best efforts: "We become what we think about." I recognized if that were true, the possibilities of what I could do with my life were limitless.

Mr. Nightingale's secret, the biblical principle "As he thinketh in his heart, so is he" (Prov. 23:7 KJV), and Norman Vincent Peale's power of positive thinking came alive to me as more than just words. Knowing this radical way of thinking would not be welcome in my house, I hid that little record under my mattress, bringing it out night after night to hear again the promises of a better life. While friends were hiding their girlie magazines under their beds, this message of hope and opportunity captured my imagination. I began to see the impact of that thinking on my belief system. Any complacency I might have held about my future disappeared forever. Yes, I attended regular public school and did well there. But my real interests were triggered by the wealth of wisdom I found in books I chose to devour.

> It is possible to store the mind with a million
> facts and still be entirely uneducated.
>
> **—ALEC BOURNE**[5]

I became intensely curious about the world and began to explore the way things worked, how they could be made better, and what possibilities existed for change and innovation. I took the lawn mower engine apart to see if I could improve its power and efficiency. I improvised new machines and inventions from old parts I salvaged from the local dump. I was drawn to the biblical stories of Joshua, Joseph, and Solomon because I saw them as examples of people who dreamed things others thought impossible and created plans of action to make their dreams a reality.

I became adept at coming up with new solutions to problems in my little world. The farming environment exposed me to carpentry, plumbing, and electrical and mechanical systems, but I began to seek out new opportunities—everything from selling Christmas cards to setting up my first roadside business—wherever I could. I saw that any developed skill had the potential to be applied for extraordinary results.

Meanwhile my infatuation with fast and fancy cars grew stronger, thanks in part to the fact that my grandparents on both sides were horse-and-buggy Amish—no cars were allowed in their households. Even when my parents decided they would have a car, the car had to be black. Some of you have undoubtedly experienced the attraction of the things that are forbidden by religious legalism.

My first car was entirely handmade. When I was eighteen years old, I purchased a 1931 Model A Ford for fifty dollars. Slowly and meticulously I began building a running street rod. Every time I found myself with an extra five dollars, instead of blowing it on candy or clothes, I went to the junkyard and bought a generator or a set of seats. I learned by doing, as well as by listening and talking to anyone who knew more than I did. Remember, I didn't have a dad who would take me into town to purchase a cool car. In our family, cars were strictly for transportation. Anything that accented visual appeal or high performance was "worldly." So while my friends conned their parents into buying them their first cars, I spent every spare minute in that unheated old chicken coop where I was building my car. One year later I drove out with an eye-stopping hot rod with a Chrysler hemi engine. This simple farm kid suddenly had a car that outshone those of most of my friends.

Seeing these simple dreams come true fueled my desire for new experiences and self-education. Upon completing high school, I was expected to become a full-time member of our family farming operation. But I wanted more, and I knew that college would help open new doors for me. Against my father's wishes, I decided to pursue college classes. I was required to help with the dairy and farming chores beginning at 5:30 a.m. But I didn't let that little detail deter me. I enrolled in a branch campus of The Ohio State University, where I could attend classes from 6:00 to 10:00 p.m.

I completed my four years at Ohio State and received a BA in psychology. After a few years of work at a psychiatric hospital, I decided to go back to school. I quit my job and my income and entered graduate school. My young but trusting wife and

I, and our first baby, lived in an old house for two years while I got a $200-a-month stipend as a teaching assistant. I got my master's degree in clinical psychology in 1975. The program cost roughly $32,000. I traded my remodeling skills in lieu of rent, and Joanne made custom-tailored clothing for hard-to-fit women. My teaching assistantship eliminated tuition fees, and we lived on essentially the $200 monthly stipend. I was able to complete this step with no student loan debt.

To show that I had successfully mastered the program, I was required to do research for and write a master's thesis. Five people read that thesis. They thought it was profound and complimented me on doing such a great job. They then gave me a really nice diploma that hangs on my wall. The completed thesis is in a nicely bound format and sits quietly on my bookshelf.

Several years later I decided to study for my doctorate. I enrolled in classes and eagerly immersed myself in the process of study once again. I completed the entire program with flying colors. Then I met with my dissertation committee, four very old guys who outlined the process. Having been through a similar scenario with my earlier degrees, I simply asked for clarification. A doctoral dissertation is not meant for reading by the common person. It must be written in a scholarly fashion with countless footnotes and references to other works. Upon completion, it would be read by these same four guys, who would then—I hoped—give me yet another really nice piece of paper to hang on my wall. At that point I summarized the options as I saw them: (1) I could spend the next 1.5 years researching and writing that cumbersome document so these old guys would be impressed enough to give me that piece of paper, or (2) I could spend the same amount of time and effort researching and writing a book that would be readable by the average person and, I hoped, make $1 million or so as a result. Much to the chagrin of those four old guys I chose option 2. The resulting book was *48 Days to the Work You Love*, and it has done exactly what I intended.[6]

I have always loved the process of study because my goal was to get the knowledge and learning, not to get a piece of paper with my name on it. I have always viewed education as something that helps increase my options, broadens my horizons, and perhaps positions me as an expert in a given field. Framing it as such, one can easily see that education can occur in many, many ways. Sitting in a classroom with thirty-two other people while regurgitating information fed from the professor may be one of the poorer methods of becoming educated.

And if you thought that getting a degree was the magic ticket to fame and fortune, you, like Chuck and Susan, may have already confronted some disappointment in the real world. The October 2, 2010, edition of *The Tennessean* stated that the average law school student now graduates with $100,000 in student loan debt. And the average starting salary for a law school graduate is $40,000. Add to that the fact that only 88 percent of the law school class of 2009 has found work of any kind in the legal field, according to the American Bar Association. And oh, yeah, there really is a book titled *Running from the Law*.[7] (You can leave your comments about this phenomenon on my blog post "Running from the Law.")[8]

I did a quick search for jobs that would be expected to pay more than $40,000:

- Taco Bell manager—$52,333
- plumbers, pipefitters, and steamfitters—$44,866
- UPS driver—$75,000
- waste management truck driver—$52,000
- nanny for Meg Whitman (former eBay CEO)—$47,840
- graphic designer—$43,560

The last I checked, none of these jobs required seven years of in-school training.

It's reasonable to add to the seven years of school the opportunity cost, meaning what was given up to spend those years sitting in a classroom. Assuming you could have gotten a job that already paid $40,000, that would add $280,000 to the $100,000 debt. And certainly the $100,000 didn't cover all the costs; perhaps another $50,000 in real money was added to the mix. So somewhere in the neighborhood of $430,000 has been invested in the process of becoming an attorney—for the opportunity of making $40,000—if you could find a job at all.

How's that for the power of an advanced degree? Okay, that's not an attractive scenario.

Yes, I talk about fulfilling and meaningful work, and you may not think some of the options I noted are that meaningful. But the most common frustration I hear from attorneys is that their work is not meaningful.

Our academic system is broken. Colleges and universities are selling a myth and false dreams. I predict we are going to see a revolution in our traditional educational system as people continue to discover alternative methods of education that *do* lead to meaningful, purposeful, and profitable work.

How many people have been affected by the fact that you have a bachelor's degree or a graduate degree of some kind? Those five guys who read my powerful master's thesis apparently didn't tell anyone else. I've never in the years since then had even one person comment on the value of that study or how it influenced her or his life in a positive way.

But I've heard from thousands of people who thank me for the hope and encouragement they received from reading *48 Days to the Work You Love*.

Not long ago I posted 48 Low-Cost Business Ideas on

48Days.net as a free download, and within the first three weeks, it had been downloaded more than ninety thousand times.[9] People tell me every day how those ideas have opened their eyes to new opportunities. Thousands of those people also went on to purchase my books and attend our live events.

> The man who is too busy to read is never likely to lead.
> —B. C. FORBES[10]

How can you make your learning change who you are and put money in your bank account? Let me share with you just some of the ways I've gotten the education I really care about—the one that has expanded my options and continues to enrich my life in many ways.

Ten Steps to Education and Becoming Rich

1. *Read (or listen to) at least twelve great books.* I have an Amazon.com Prime membership with unlimited free two-day shipping, and I buy books liberally. I encourage you to do the same. However, if you feel you cannot invest even small dollars in your education, check the books out of the library. (See the complete list here: Dan's Reading List.)[11]

   I know of no way to more quickly change your level of success than to read good books. Try these:

   - Old Classics
     - *Think and Grow Rich* (Napoleon Hill)
     - *The Magic of Thinking Big* (David J. Schwartz, PhD)

- *How to Win Friends and Influence People* (Dale Carnegie)
- *The Strangest Secret* (Earl Nightingale)

- Timeless Greats
  - *Thou Shall Prosper* (Daniel Lapin)
  - *A Whole New Mind* (Daniel H. Pink)
  - *How to Think Like Leonardo da Vinci* (Michael J. Gelb)
  - *The Success Principles* (Jack Canfield and Janet Switzer)

- More Recent Titles
  - *Trust Agents* (Chris Brogan and Julien Smith)
  - *Linchpin* (Seth Godin)
  - *The Compound Effect* (Darren Hardy)
  - *The Art of Non-Conformity* (Chris Guillebeau)

Just a note of clarification: I have read many books (seventy-eight in 2011) and love the continued adding of knowledge, stretching of my thinking, and stimulating of new ideas. Please do not discard the entire contents of a book if you find a principle or theological premise with which you do not agree. No one burns down a house if he finds a mouse. Just eliminate the mouse and continue to enjoy the other rich features of the house.

I find television very educational. Every time somebody turns it on, I go into the other room and read a book.

—GROUCHO MARX[12]

2. *Attend three or four seminars.* Choose what you'd like but go with an open mind. I attend a lot of seminars each year. My goal is not to change my life with any one seminar but to learn at least one great idea that I can use from each one.

- No More Mondays Cruise: various speakers[13]
- Storyline: Donald Miller[14]
- Speakers' Boot Camp: Kent Julian[15]
- TED Conference: various speakers[16]
- Coaching with Excellence: Dan Miller and Ashley Miller Logsdon[17]
- Global Leadership Summit: Willow Creek Association[18]
- Write to the Bank: Dan and Joanne Miller[19]
- Local community workshops and seminars (check weekly listings)

Every now and then a man's mind is stretched by a new idea or sensation, and never shrinks back to its former dimensions.
—OLIVER WENDELL HOLMES SR.[20]

3. *Subscribe to at least two great magazines.* You can get almost any magazine online if you prefer. I still enjoy holding the magazine, turning the pages, and returning to them again and again. Consider these:

- *Success* (includes an audio CD each month— invaluable)[21]

- *Fast Company*[22]
- *Inc.*[23]
- *Wired*[24]
- *Entrepreneur*[25]
- *Ode*[26]

Learning is a treasure that will follow
its owner everywhere.

—CHINESE PROVERB

4. *Listen to three or four informational podcasts, and read three or four blogs each week.* You may be an auditory or visual learner. No right or wrong here. Just select what works for you. The free information is priceless.

- Dan Miller: *48 Days*[27]
- Guy Kawasaki: *How to Change the World*[28]
- Seth Godin: *Seth's Blog*[29]
- Chris Guillebeau: *The Art of Non-Conformity*[30]
- Jon Acuff: *Stuff Christians Like*[31]
- Michael Hyatt: *Intentional Leadership*[32]

5. *Get involved in a social networking community* like 48Days.net. I'm also a member of Triiibes.com, RansomedHeart.net, and FreeAgentAcademy.[33] Find a couple where you can identify with the group, and then get involved. Contribute, ask questions, and give advice. You'll find your center of influence will grow rapidly.

- Start your own blog. It's free on WordPress[34], or you can just jump into the community at 48Days.net.
- Write and then comment on others' blogs.

6. *Reach out to help someone else.*

- Loan money to an entrepreneur through Kiva.[35] These are people around the world who are committed to living a better story. Helping them will help you feel connected to a larger life than what you have now. And it will likely cost you zero dollars since 98 percent of the loans are repaid. You can do this again and again. I recently loaned fifty dollars to a guy in Ecuador who is an auto mechanic and wanted to expand his tool supply. And then I made another loan to a woman in Peru who has her own little Laundromat. She has two washing machines now and allows the village women to come in and do their laundry. She wants to add two more machines to expand her little business. I saw the loans being repaid with amounts like $3.47 a month. Both loans have now been totally repaid, and I can provide those funds for others finding their own success. I enjoy being part of these stories.
- Provide a goat and two chickens for one hundred dollars through World Vision.[36] You'll be giving a precious start to a family seeking to improve their lives.
- Volunteer for a Habitat for Humanity house project.
- Mentor an ex-felon who needs a hand up (Leaving the Cocoon, Men of Valor).[37]

7. *Acquire at least one new skill this year.* Each year I
   select an area of interest having nothing to do with
   business or making money. Purely for the education.
   Imagine that.

   - Discover photography.
   - Learn martial arts.
   - Investigate astronomy.
   - Explore our spiritual heritage.
   - Catalog birds in your local area.
   - Learn a new language.
   - Take the *Drawing on the Right Side of the Brain* class
     (based on a book by Betty Edwards).
   - Start a book discussion or Mastermind group.
   - Get a vocational degree in something you can use
     immediately.

> Anyone who stops learning is old—
> whether at twenty or eighty.
> **—HENRY FORD**[38]

8. *Become comfortable with your presentation skills.*
   No matter what your career or business you must
   be comfortable presenting your ideas. It will do
   wonders for your confidence and self-esteem. You
   will find it easier to complete a sales transaction,
   have conversations with family and friends, and
   find success in your career.

- Join Toastmasters.[39]
- Take the Dale Carnegie Human Relations course (free first session).[40]
- Teach a Sunday school class at your church.
- Volunteer to lead a book discussion at your local library.

9. *Design your own health and fitness program.* Success is never just about making money. If you deplete your physical resources, you will fail at everything else. Make sure you are making deposits of success in this area every day.

- Join a club.
- Design your own plan.
- Read two great nutrition books.
- Control your diet.
- Make good choices consistently.

10. *Plan two trips this year.* Many people think they cannot afford to travel. Joanne and I have continued to travel even through our toughest times financially. I've been treating her to Christmastime in Chicago for more than twenty years now. Direct flights from Nashville used to be sixty-nine dollars round trip (a little more now). And few people travel on business the week of Christmas so four-star hotels are cheap and easy to get. Typically I have used Priceline.com to put in my bid of about seventy-nine dollars a night. But just do something that excites you. Be creative. Joanne and I often go to downtown Nashville and pretend we're tourists. We

walk through the classic churches, over the unique pedestrian bridges, and visit the art exhibits.

- Choose to go off-season (for example, Chicago at Christmastime).
- Swap houses with someone anywhere in the world, or rent a unique place from the owner (like a cottage in Ireland for $280 a week).[41]
- Try Vacation Rentals by Owner.[42]

I'm sure you could probably add more examples of experiences in your life that have helped you get an education. With today's technology you can listen to your iPod while cleaning the house or driving your car. (Speaking of driving time, join the Automobile University. If you drive twenty-five thousand miles a year at an average speed of forty-six miles per hour, you will spend about the same amount of time in your car as an average college student spends in the classroom. The question then is, what are you doing with that time? You can listen to CDs and transform your success.) You can take a long nature walk and really *see* your surroundings. I often take a walk on our property with coaching clients. If that person misses the squirrels, the deer, the butterflies, the waterfall, and the setting sun, I have a pretty clear picture of why he or she is also unconnected socially, physically, and spiritually.

Never become so much of an expert that you stop gaining expertise. View life as a continuous learning experience.
—DENIS WAITLEY[43]

Education Around the World

Elizabeth Dearborn Davis moved to Rwanda a few days after graduating from Vanderbilt University in Nashville, Tennessee. She joined a Global Youth Connect delegation to study post-conflict reconciliation and human rights advocacy.[44] She stayed in Rwanda to volunteer with grassroots education projects and in 2007 founded a nonprofit organization to provide scholarships to street children and to support an orphanage in Kigali. The idea for Akilah Institute for Women first developed in 2008.[45]

Elizabeth has worked on education and community development projects in Costa Rica, Ecuador, Peru, and South Africa. She was a founding member of Students for Kenya, an organization supporting the Lwala Health Clinic in western Kenya. At Vanderbilt, she was the president of STAND (the student-led division of the Genocide Intervention Network) and a cofounder of Fashion for a Cause. In 2008, she was selected as a StartingBloc Fellow.[46] Elizabeth received the Woman of Peace award from the Women's Peace Power Foundation in October 2009. She was selected as a speaker at TEDx Tampa Bay in February 2010.[47]

The Akilah Institute opened in Kigali with its first class of fifty girls in February 2010. Akilah offers a two-year business diploma with a focus in hospitality management or entrepreneurship. A team of education and development experts from Johnson & Wales University, Vanderbilt University, the Rwanda Private Sector Federation, the Ministry of Education, and an advisory council of industry leaders in Rwanda developed the two-year curriculum. The curriculum is a direct response to the needs of the private sector, and the courses combine classroom instruction, based on proven training models, with entrepreneurial skills. It challenges students with real-world opportunities to be involved in the daily realities of running a small business.

Elizabeth has also partnered with the new Hilton Hotel being built in Kigali, Rwanda. They will provide internships for all students and immediate employment for graduates of the Akilah Institute.

That's education with a purpose.

> An educational system isn't worth a great deal
> if it teaches young people how to make a living
> but doesn't teach them how to make a life.
>
> **—AUTHOR UNKNOWN**

The Educated Unemployed

I'll bet you can name ten people with fancy college degrees who are struggling to find work right now. Or they just took the difficulty as a reason to go back and get another degree—confident that if they have another piece of paper, someone will *give* them a job.

Do you know that our universities are graduating exactly ten times more psychology majors each year than there are jobs for psychology majors?[48] But are college guidance counselors telling these bright-eyed kids, "There will be a job for only one in every ten of you; the rest of you will have to figure out some other way to repay your student loans and make a living"? Of course not. We encourage even more to get that

degree in psychology, political science, graphic design, or, for the chronically indecisive, university studies.

Okay, schools are trying to adjust. You can now get a degree in these fields[49]:

- Packaging—University of Wisconsin-Stout
- Viticulture and enology—Cornell University
- Puppetry—University of Connecticut
- Decision making—Kelley School of Business, Indiana University
- Turfgrass management—Michigan State University
- Master ranching—Texas A&M
- Retail floristry—Mississippi State University
- Professional nanny—Sullivan University

Do we really need four-year degrees to be an expert in these areas?

Of course if you are unsure about a clear focus, you can take these classes (yes, these are all real class offerings): the Art of Walking, Maple Syrup, Tightwaddery, the American Vacation, Finding Dates Worth Keeping, the Amazing World of Bubbles, or Alien Sex.

Is it any wonder we have growing numbers of educated unemployed in our ranks?

He who has learning without imagination
has feet but no wings.
—STANLEY GOLDSTEIN[50]

Oh, yes, as I mentioned, I have a BA in psychology and an MA in clinical psychology. Very enjoyable studies and I learned a lot about myself. And then I figured out how to make a living.

What in your training or experience makes you employable? What value do you bring to the table—whether or not you have a degree?

Maybe you just need to add imagination to your education.

Adding imagination to our learning can put wings on our possibilities.

I did not do well in the formal education atmosphere. I struggled in class because I am dyslexic, so I read slowly. And frankly I was just bored. Not a good combo.

However, I usually had a great rapport with my teachers because I took the time to create a relationship with them. So I squeaked through homeschooling and tutoring to get a high school diploma, largely due to a few wise teachers who recognized my creativity and desire to do and be more. (Thank you, Diane West, for believing in me.)

I honestly don't remember a thing in terms of academics from high school. I didn't even complete prealgebra. But I do remember the relationships I created. I have friends from that time that I still talk to weekly, even when I am in Africa. They are like family, and most have been for more than fifteen years. I'd say that's the most valuable aspect of my formal education.

I've always believed in learning application over theory. I can read something in a book ten times, taking months to dissect it, and still not have the understanding I would have from ten minutes of application.

When I wanted to learn the music industry, I tracked

down Bill Miller, a Mohican musician whom I was really into at the time. Bill represented a lot of things I wanted to be, and I loved his music (still do). So I found a connection to his daughter, got his manager's phone number, got rejected four times, and finally found his office and waited on his doorstep at lunchtime.

I think Bill and his staff were about ready to call the police, but I politely asked for one lunch with them and then promised to leave them alone. They agreed, and we headed off to the famous 12th & Porter in downtown Nashville, a popular musician lunch spot.

They had no job for me, no budget to pay me, and didn't know me from Adam. Forty-five minutes later I had a job working for a musician with whom I was completely enthralled—on Music Row! Over the next eight months, I gained the foundational tools I needed to work my way into the industry. I was in a sink-or-swim situation and knew I had to learn quickly, so I did.

Eight months later I tried the same technique with one of MCA/Universal Records' most respected A&R reps. She had picked singles for Led Zeppelin back in the day and was still calling the shots for their biggest artists. She had no job or budget for me. But I convinced her to let me sit in her office for a few days. A couple weeks later I got my first gig. She sent me to Little Rock, Arkansas, to check out a new band called Blue October,[51] all expenses paid. I was in heaven.

I could list countless opportunities I've created over the years. I went straight to the top and learned everything I could, in application, not just from theory in a book or classroom. I always knew that I had the charisma, confidence, drive, discipline, and problem-solving skills to figure out any situation I might encounter. So I just went for it, again and again.

Consequently, over the years, I've built a car, worked for the man who developed mountain biking (Tom Ritchey), remodeled houses, worked as a gourmet chef, managed rock bands, held massive concerts, managed an Amish furniture company, co-owned a pro bicycle shop, built an airplane (yep), written and passed a law to criminalize the solicitation of prostitution in Rwanda, created my own ethical fashion label, lectured at universities, spoken at countless churches, lived with Maasai warriors in the bush of Kenya and Tanzania, created the first annual mountain bike race in Rwanda, consulted for the governments of Nigeria and Rwanda, created the Swahili Coast Fashion Group, and undertaken countless other adventures.

Along the way I've met some of the most extraordinary people. Many of them are major celebrities, world leaders, powerful politicians, and similarly successful and influential icons. I never had a bit of formal education that prepared or qualified me for these things. I simply believed in my abilities to figure out things. I've always relied heavily on my dedication to problem solving. If I get into a difficult situation or something I don't understand, I know myself well enough to know I won't stop until I figure it out. And I'll do it with excellence.

I've always believed in asking lots of questions. If I see something I don't know how to do, I'll stop and watch someone else who is doing it well, or do the research to find someone or some resource I can learn from. Anything is possible when you're willing to put in the effort and believe in yourself.

When asked what school I attended, my mother usually says, "He went to the school of life." This is true. And fortunately I was able to major in about eighty-five subjects, and the education is ongoing. I am frequently asked to speak at universities on the issues of development in Africa, branding, gender-based violence policies, women's rights, and more effective philanthropy strategies. Never once has someone asked for my qualifications or diploma. People just assumed I had been formally trained. Au contraire.

You can get your education for free anytime you want it. Get online. Apprentice somewhere. Believe in yourself, and don't be afraid to fail. Your failures are typically the stepping-stones to your greatest successes.

Does Education Expand or Limit Your Options?

Of course we assume that any degree expands our possibilities. Someone with an MD behind her name certainly has far more options than someone without a graduate degree or even a BA. A person with any college degree has more opportunity than a person who has never invested the time, energy, and money to get that valuable piece of paper. Or does he?

Some of the most difficult clients I encounter have multiple advanced degrees. What happens in times of change is that they view their options as very limited. The dentist sees his only option as continuing the practice of dentistry, even if he hates every single day and has failed miserably in prospering financially. The attorney assumes her only choice is to continue in law, even though she knows she went to law school for all the wrong reasons.

There is a principle called *beginner's mind* that implies if your mind is empty, it is always ready for anything; it is open to everything. To extend this a little, in the beginner's mind there are many possibilities; in the expert's mind there are few.

In times of change those with a beginner's mind see opportunities to realign their skills into new opportunities. The former web designer is now a social media consultant; the dentist starts a buying co-op for his profession; the medical doctor pursues his invention for breathable baby mattresses; and the college dropout starts an adventure travel business.

"Experts" are often immobilized. They struggle with imagining new possibilities. They are trapped into narrow thinking with their fancy degrees and miss the opportunities emerging all around them.

Make sure you keep a beginner's mind. Watch a four-year-old for a day or two. Observe how she approaches a box of blocks or a walk down the lane. Don't let your education blind you to uncomplicated possibilities.

We have a very extensive international intern program at our fashion label (KEZA) here in Kenya.[52] We bring in students from all around the world to learn how to work, develop, design, and operate effectively in Africa.

Over the years we've developed systems for helping interns acclimate to the culture and understand how to truly serve Africa in the way it needs. Through this process we've noticed that we usually spend the first two months of a four-month internship attempting to help our interns unlearn most of what they've been taught at their university or through social conditioning.

I've also noticed that we do a lot of this with the artisans and entrepreneurs we work with right here in Africa. They had many years of education learning how to obey, not to think. I've resolved that we can be the best asset to Africa by just teaching people how to think.

I see so many aid agencies teaching skills and method-ologies on how to run a business, operate a farm, manage a school, and carry out many other initiatives. But the most powerful and effective programs are the ones that help people unlearn bad habits and self-doubt and actually teach them to think and be problem solvers. When are the aid agencies and academic institutions going to create a problem-solving major?

When I'm hiring an employee or accepting an intern application, especially for a position of leadership, I don't care about academic education. I don't even ask about it. What I do care about is someone's ability to be a self-starter, to think outside the box, to establish solid relationships, to maintain healthy self-confidence, and to be a problem solver. Unfortunately I've not seen any college courses that develop and foster this type of mentality.

What I do see is a lot of formal education systems that are churning out drones incapable of thinking out-side the textbook they just spent four years studying. These graduates are going to spend the next ten years having to unlearn the majority of what they just spent $30,000 to $150,000 on for education. Seems a bit ironic and self-destructive.

Gretchen Ain't No Dummy

With a troubled home life, Gretchen Wilson, known for the song "Redneck Woman," dropped out of school in the ninth grade and never went back. Although that didn't stop her from her musical success, she was concerned about being a role model for her daughter. In April 2008, Gretchen passed her GED exam and wore a cap and gown for the May 15 graduation ceremony at Wilson County High School in Tennessee. "It's not one of the requirements you have to have to become a star," said Joe Galante, chairman of her label, Sony BMG Nashville.[53]

What's up with that? How common is it for someone to knock it outta the park without having a college degree? Well, it turns out it is very common. Here are some findings from a study by the Harrison Group on the top half of the top 1 percent of America's wealthiest individuals—those with assets of $5 million and more:

• Entrepreneurs are less likely to be college graduates than nonentrepreneurs.
• They are more likely to attribute their success to determination, while nonentrepreneurs credit intelligence and education.
• They say their happiness increases as they accumulate more money.
• They are more likely to say money brings them self-confidence, while nonentrepreneurs say money brings them security.[54]

In *The Millionaire Next Door* coauthors Thomas Stanley and William Danko said that most of the millionaires they studied had been told by some authority figure that they were not

• intellectually gifted,
• of law school caliber,
• medical school material,
• qualified to pursue an MBA degree, or
• smart enough to succeed.[55]

As I wrote in *No More Dreaded Mondays*, it appears the critical characteristics for becoming successful are (1) passion, (2) determination, (3) talent, (4) self-discipline, and (5) faith.[56] With those in place, degrees pale in importance.

Cramming for College—and Life as a Robot

An article in *Fast Company* titled "Cramming for College at Beijing's Second High" describes the current process of students in Beijing preparing for the gaokao, the national college-entrance exams, "which are seen as the gateway to success in life."[57]

Students cram for the answers required by the exam's authors. "The gaokao rewards a special type of student: very strong memory; very strong logical and analytical ability; little imagination; little desire to question authority," says Jiang Xueqin, a Yale-educated school administrator in Beijing.

I cringed as I read about a typical week for a high school student: "He rises before dawn to be at school by 7:30 a.m., six days a week. After school lets out at 5 p.m.—he studies at least five hours more."

Wow! I think about my life in high school. The moment school was dismissed I jumped into farm chores. I had done the minimum in school and needed to work in the family business. Was that depriving me of an education? Or was that an opportunity to dream, explore, imagine, experiment with new inventions, and learn about the weather, mechanics, electricity, plumbing, and carpentry? What about Saturdays when I rode bikes with my friends, played ball, and chased girls? Was that time wasted while I could have been cramming my brain full of facts, figures, and information that would help me on a standardized test?

Chinese (and American) students often end up with high-level degrees and no meaningful life. There must be a balance between accumulating knowledge and developing fulfilling relationships. I am gravely concerned about what has happened in the United States with our own chasing of degrees as opposed to getting an education rich in experiences, imagination, and relationships. When I watch my granddaughters revealing their dreams with paint and canvas, dressing in magical dresses, talking to the goats, or catching tiny frogs in our pond, I know they are discovering personal passions that will lead to an exciting and purposeful future.

No one should have to cram so hard that real life gets crowded out. The challenge is to be raising creative, unique individuals, not robots.

Education in Your House

So how are you getting your education? Perhaps no one will be looking over your shoulder or giving you a grade. But your life will display the "grade" you've given yourself. Let me know about your As in the coming year. Join the discussions with others who are creating the future they want at 48Days.net.

> The man who is too old to learn was probably always too old to learn.
>
> **—HENRY S. HASKINS**[58]

Update: We invited "Chuck" and "Susan" to our sanctuary for a Coaching with Excellence weekend event with other learners. They were apologetic about the anger directed my way and very appreciative of our ongoing care and concern. They absorbed the weekend teachings and explored additional options. I received a note a few days later: "We have a renewed sense of confidence, excitement, and hope now as we seek the next step on our journey. Thank you so much for choosing to go above and beyond for us at this challenging and crucial time in our lives."

CHAPTER FOUR

Lemonade Stand or Facebook

When Mark Zuckerberg was twenty-four years old, he turned down $1 billion for the little network he created called Facebook. *Time* magazine named him Person of the Year in 2010 and described his indifference to money as "almost pathological." If money doesn't drive a person in business, what does? New factors like being green and socially responsible appear to be more attractive concepts for today's growing entrepreneurs.

IMPACT OR ACCOLADES?

When Ilea and I were running our fashion company (KEZA) in Rwanda, people were chomping at the bit to work with us. Why? Rwanda has been a hotbed for conflict in the past. It's right next to the Democratic Republic of the Congo (DRC), another hot zone. These places are sexy to budding activists. People who work in these areas are regarded as better, more caring human beings; revolutionaries.

To be a good humanitarian, you must sacrifice, suffer, and live in a conflict zone.

Or you could dig a little deeper.

Over the past six years of living in East Africa, I've learned that more than anything, Africa wants more business, not more aid. I've also learned that attempting to build solid businesses with the poorest of the poor in the middle of a conflict zone is not the most logical path to business development. Providing entrepreneurs with the skills, determination, and experience to lead thriving businesses has proven to be a much more successful method. As their businesses grow, their success tends to trickle down to the poorest of the poor, offering more jobs and infrastructure along the way. Furthermore, finding these entrepreneurs in the midst of conflict areas is nearly impossible. These people are struggling just to survive, and there's no infrastructure or resources to support them. Their businesses are sabotaged daily by all sorts of outside forces.

A few years ago we decided to move to Mombasa, Kenya, not necessarily known for conflict. It's a tourist beach town on the Indian Ocean. It's beautiful and magical, and thousands of tourists flock here annually. It's also ripe for business development. The business conditions are far from ideal, but compared to some of the hot zones I've lived in, it's pretty optimal. When we develop a business here, it really has the opportunity to thrive and have an impact on larger communities for the long haul.

But guess what? Many former supporters have turned their attention elsewhere. Interns are not as attracted to our work because life here doesn't seem sacrificial enough. Never mind the potential for impact.

When you say you live and work in Africa, people expect you should be dodging hand grenades in order to be effective. Not so. There's a time and place for that, but it's not very conducive for business development.

Africa wants business. Business makes the world turn, like it or not. The Western/developed world isn't perfect. But there are a lot fewer people dying of starvation and disease there. And the developed world wasn't built on aid; it was built on solid businesses.

If you wanted to assemble a football team that would raise up a nation, you'd find the best players in the best area and go for it. Or you could pick the least qualified players in an area with insurmountable obstacles. Doing the latter may earn you lots of praise, but it's not likely to produce the desired results.

If the nation is depending on the team, why not put your best foot forward for the country? This approach is not as likely to earn you accolades, but it might be more effective.

I guess at that point you just have to question your true motivation: impact or accolades?

Poverty or Simplicity

The current recession or economic downturn has prompted many people to enjoy a healthier, greener, more ecologically responsible, and simpler lifestyle. So what is the difference between poverty and simplicity?

If I'm angry that I can't afford a new Ferrari, I may feel I've been doomed to poverty. However, if I enjoy the classic lines and character of a twenty-year-old sports car I can easily afford, then it appears I have chosen simplicity. If I "can't afford" to eat at Ruth's Chris, I may begrudge the government's tax and economic policies. If Joanne and I invite friends over for a pot-luck dinner where our contribution comes from our neighbor's garden-grown cucumbers and tomatoes, our peace of mind may originate from our choice for simplicity.

John Robbins, author of *Diet for a New America* and *The Food Revolution*, turned down his family's Baskin-Robbins ice-cream fortune in order to "live a far more simple and Earth-friendly life." He and his wife built a tiny, one-room log cabin on an island off the coast of British Columbia, where they grow most of their own food. John says, "This isn't about deprivation. It's about choice and self-determination."[1]

On the TV show *Living with Ed*, the goal is for Ed Begley Jr. to show us how to have the lowest possible carbon footprint and get the most efficient use of energy and resources possible. Although a successful actor, Ed chooses to ride his bicycle nearly everywhere he goes. Ed has it right with his one simple phrase: "Live simply . . . so others can simply live."[2]

The dictionary defines *poverty* as "the state of being poor; lack of the means of providing material needs or comforts." The definition of *simplicity* is "the absence of luxury, pretentious-ness, ornament, etc."[3]

Could it be that whether we live in poverty or simplicity is primarily a choice of how we view our situation? Simplicity has many rewards that go beyond saving money. Among those may be the experience of living well.

From the first time I saw *We Are the World* on MTV in 1985,[4] I was hooked on Africa. I was six at the time. I dreamed of coming to Africa to help. I had no idea of the journey that would unfold as I followed that dream.

As the years passed, my attention was consistently focused on learning more and more about Africa. I was enthralled with the culture, the people, the stunning landscapes, and the deep history. I'm also mesmerized and awed by the sea. I love the coastal culture, and for me there is no greater representation of God's power and creativity in nature than the full moon reflecting off the sea, palm trees swaying in the wind. Utter bliss.

This love of the coast combined with my love for Africa naturally led me to Mombasa, Kenya. It's the culmination of everything I love about Africa and specifically the Swahili culture.[5] *Swahili* is actually an Arabic word meaning "coastal dwellers" and has now defined a people, region, language, and rich culture.

I did not grow up in a financially well-off family. However, I did grow up in a family that fostered the idea that we are to dream big and believe in our ability to make manifest those dreams. Since I was sixteen, my dream has been to live on the beach in Mombasa. Eighteen years later, here I am.

Ilea and I married on May 8, 2010. We sat down and said, "We are going to believe this Mombasa dream into fruition; we'll make it manifest, despite all of the odds against us." We had no money, no concrete plan, and very little income. Less than one year later, we were sitting on our balcony, overlooking the sea.

This morning, I woke at 6:30 a.m. as usual and stood outside as I sipped my coffee and took it all in. We live in a quaint little two-bedroom, one-bath flat on the third (top) floor. We have an amazing flat rooftop where Francois and I spend our nights stargazing with our telescope (thank you, Ilea and family!). We have a beautifully landscaped common area for a front yard that leads right up to the beach. We have twenty-four large tropical plants in multicolored clay pots that Ilea and I painted together.

The mornings are filled with sounds of exotic birds, geckos (yes, they make noises), monkeys, cranes, ocean waves, and nothing else. The afternoons are quiet, and the breeze flows soothingly through the house all day. In the evenings, our home is filled with the ever-present symphony of laughter, children, and talking from families and visitors on the beach, only fifty yards away. I never tire of that song.

Our home has a new coat of brilliant white from top to bottom, with a few blue, fuchsia, and teal accent walls. We have no furniture other than a mattress that lies on some old pallets and grass mats, draped in a custom mosquito net that I designed for our room. It's the perfect blank canvas to paint our story and create what my mother calls "a haven of peace."

We keep looking at each other and saying, "Hey, this is where we live. We're not just on vacation!" We are constantly in awe of it all.

We do the work we love and are passionate about. We have purpose. We have a beautiful marriage. And we recently landed the most lucrative (and one of the most fulfilling) consulting contract we've ever received. Francois, too, loves the Mombasa life. And we've got a little Angaza due in a few months.

In some ways, our lives today seem surreal. But as I contemplate it more this morning, I realize again that this is how our lives were designed to unfold. We were created to live this way, and we've made choices that are congruent with that flow. Consequently, we live very happy and ful-filled lives.

At each step of the way, we deliberately chose to believe that we could achieve this. We chose not to let fear conquer us. We chose to believe in abundance, that we'll always have more than what we need. We believe in each other. And we believe that the universe and our Creator are always working for us, not against us.

We chose this life. We didn't let doubts and social norms stop us from bringing it into fruition. We got out of the way and let it come to us. And now it's here.

The life we live here is definitely simple. Life in Kenya is very different from life in the United States. It's raw and always keeps us on our toes. I've always said, "If you want something in Africa, you've really got to want it bad. Otherwise, it's not going to happen."

You have to be very deliberate about everything. Life doesn't just fall into your lap. The power goes out, the house gets flooded, we run out of water, no one is on time, transportation is rough, and there are lots of other variables that come into play every day.

If I want a new shelf or ceiling fans or a new couch, I have to work hard to make it happen. There is no Ikea or Target to walk into. It took us three weeks to find ceiling fans, which we painted to match the room. I designed our mosquito net to fit our every need, and now I'm designing our couch and dining table. It will take me a few weeks to design them, find the wood, find the fabric and insides for the cushions, find a guy with the tools and know-how, and negotiate the price, and then I'll spend a few more weeks managing the process.

Everything we have here has been created that way. We appreciate everything we have so much because we worked so hard to get it. For the same reason, we take care of things as if they were family heirlooms.

Life here keeps us on our toes for sure, and we love it. Often we'll have friends over to watch a movie on our computer screen or hang out, and right in the middle, the power goes out. And there we are with nothing left to do but talk in the dark. We go up on the roof or out to the beach and chat away about things that likely would have never come up if the power hadn't gone out.

When the power finally comes back on, I'm reminded of how grateful I am that I can take a shower after a long day in ninety-eight-degree weather. So many around me don't have that luxury. When I drive through Bombolulu, a suburb of Mombasa, in the rain on my way to town, I am reminded of how grateful I am that we have a car and don't have to walk through five inches of mud just to go to lunch or get home.

I love that I live in a place that never lets me be ungrateful or forget the beauty of my surroundings. Things are extreme here. And after many years of living here, I'm also grateful that I've learned to take this reality with me everywhere in the world that I go.

The simplicity and rawness make me the man I want to be: aware, grateful, and patient.

Small Wages. Bitter Cold. Long Months . . .

"Men wanted for hazardous journey. Small wages. Bitter cold. Long months of complete darkness . . ." This ad was placed in the early 1900s by the explorer Ernest Shackleton as he was looking for men to help him discover the South Pole. The ad drew more than five thousand brave candidates.[6]

> Do not follow where the path may lead. Go
> instead where there is no path and leave a trail.
>
> **—GEORGE BERNARD SHAW**[7]

Are you looking for a safe and stable position today? One that is secure, predictable, and nonthreatening? Then maybe you're missing the best opportunities. I truly believe that if defeat or failure is not possible, then winning will not be very sweet.

Today I see fresh college graduates holding out for signing bonuses, guaranteed salaries, benefits, pensions, and stock options before agreeing to work with a company. I see guys who lost a $120,000 job and are turning down an $80,000 job because it's not what "they're worth" or not a secure position. What is a secure and stable position in today's workplace? General Douglas MacArthur said that security is one's ability to produce.[8] Knowing what you do well is your only security. It doesn't come from a company, the government, or your union.

> Security is mostly a superstition. It does not
> exist in nature, nor do the children of men as a
> whole experience it. . . . Avoiding danger is no
> safer in the long run than outright exposure.
> Life is either a daring adventure or nothing.
>
> **—HELEN KELLER**[9]

A missionary society wrote to David Livingstone deep in the heart of Africa and asked, "Have you found a good road to where you are? If so, we want to know how to send other men to help you." Livingstone wrote back: "If you have men who will come only if they know there is a good road, I don't want them. I want men who will come if there is no road at all."[10]

In times of volatility, welcome the possibility of positive new change and challenge. Looking for security may be keeping you from a higher level of success and fulfillment.

Is the quest for security keeping you from seeing new and better opportunities?

Hourly Pay Will Keep You Poor

In challenging times I see people managing their money better. And I commend them on getting involved with programs such as Dave Ramsey's Financial Peace University, as thousands have already done.[11] But here's an important principle: not only is it important to manage your money better; it's also important to realize that now is a great time to figure out how to make more money.

Wealth isn't made by the hour; it's made with ideas and a plan of action.

If you make $15 an hour, you're making $31,000 a year. A cost of living increase of 3 to 4 percent is not going to significantly change your financial position. Yes, you can do a great job and ask for a 10 percent raise each year, and in eight years you'll double your income to $62,000. But that's eight years from now. And doubling your pay in an hourly position is not going to happen unless you bring new skills to the table.

A better question is, how can you make an extra $2,600 a month starting now to make that doubling of your income be a reality this year? What would that do to your debt snowball? Here are some ideas to get your thinking started:

- Mow ten yards weekly at $60 each.
- Spend $1,300 on old silver at garage and estate sales; clean it up, know the market, and double your investment selling on eBay.
- Create a sports-themed sticker package for golf carts, and sell one hundred at $26 each.
- Be the graffiti removal expert in your town. Get ten contracts for $260 monthly to keep a building graffiti free.
- Set up to sell kettle corn at local fairs, festivals, fund-raisers, and church events. Book three events a month where you could reasonably expect to net $850 each.
- Explore the list of my 48 Low-Cost Business Ideas.[12]

Nothing here requires another degree or a waiting time. But making an idea work for you does require a break from a paycheck mentality. If you can do that, the sky is the limit in where your income can go this year.

Unlock Your Best Ideas—Here's How . . .

Here's a common question from one of my 48 Days podcast[13] listeners and perhaps similar to your thinking as well: "Dan, I feel like I've lost my creativity. My work has sucked all the juices out of me. Do you have any ideas on how to get the creative juices flowing again? I can't even sit down and think of my hobbies. What if I can't think of anything I would 'love' to do?"

Here are some tips to unlock your creativity:

- "Sit" longer.
- Get away from your normal routine.
- Go for a long walk; exercise more.

- Take an art (woodworking, sculpture, or gardening) class.
- Be around people who are high performers.
- Put yourself in a completely different environment that stretches your comfort zone.

Henry Ford once said he didn't want executives who had to work all the time. He insisted that those who were always in a flurry of activity at their desks were not being the most productive. He wanted people who would clear their desks, prop their feet up, and dream some fresh dreams. His philosophy was that only he who has the luxury of time can originate a creative thought.[14]

Wow! When was the last time your boss told you to quit working and do more dreaming? Unfortunately our culture glamorizes being under time pressure. Having too much to do with too little time is a badge of success. Or is it?

I heard from a gentleman who has spent the last three years living in an isolated old farmhouse and hiking. He said he had experienced the "perfect storm"—divorce, unfulfilling job, nasty boss, and a thirty-three-year dream of hiking the Appalachian Trail. After he spent three years "sitting," his thinking is now clear, his energy is renewed, his anger is gone, his creativity has been revived, and he is ready to map out the next season of his life.

The apostle Paul took long walks between cities, using the time to think and talk. Even when shipwrecked, instead of calling in a helicopter to get him to his next gig, he used the unexpected time to create with his mind. The philosopher and inventor Elmer Gates would go into an empty room for hours at a time, not allowing any interruptions, as he was "sitting for ideas."[15]

Thomas Edison would go down to the water's edge each morning, throw out his line—with no bait—and then watch the bobber for an hour until his thinking was ready for the day.[16] Without taking long walks, an hour here and there of bush hogging, tinkering with my cars, or playing with a grandchild, my writing to bring inspiration to others would very quickly be reduced to dry theories and lifeless words.

If you are feeling stuck, your solution may not be in doing more, but in taking a break from the busyness of life. Want to be more productive? Try doing less. Go sit somewhere awhile!

Have you spent time recently sitting for ideas?

How could you do less this week and perhaps unleash your greatest idea?

Two years ago Ilea and I spent a year traveling through the United States in order to create and foster strategic relationships that would help us build our fashion label. We also spent a lot of time with family, knowing we were gearing up to head to Kenya to put down some roots and raise a family. We also did a lot of soul-searching and deliberate thinking about how we wanted to raise a family and where. The time was very productive and certainly played a vital role in getting us where we are today.

Much like my other family members, I love to write. It's quite therapeutic for me and always helps me to expand my thinking and grow new ideas.

While in the United States, we were traveling around from city to city meeting with people, setting up vendor relationships, promoting KEZA, and so on. And while it wasn't easy, it was definitely a lot easier than our life in Africa. Eating was easy and quick, transportation was easy and reliable, accommodations were quite nice, we had a big network of great friends and family to take care of us, and in general, life just sort of rolled by.

Over the course of thirteen months, I think I squeaked out one solitary blog. I don't even remember what it was about. I tried to write more, but I always found myself too busy, too stressed, too tired, or something along those lines. What I didn't find is that I was feeling too creative.

The creative juices just weren't flowing. Life was too easy, and it didn't force me to problem solve or look at life through a different lens. I didn't feel challenged, and I was in the same easy environment that always sort of sets me on autopilot.

However, the second we stepped off the plane onto African soil, I felt a wave of creativity come over me. I wrote four of my best blogs in the first week that we were visiting my old stomping grounds in Rwanda. Then we made it to Mombasa and I haven't stopped writing since.

Environment matters. I like to be in a place that challenges me, keeps me on my toes, forces me to problem solve, and pushes my ability to create. Africa does that for me. And on top of that, it's one of the most beautiful, awe-inspiring places in the world.

I know that I need to create an environment around me that optimizes my creativity, and I know exactly what that environment looks like. I've collected little attributes and elements along the way as I've searched for that optimal environment. It's different for everyone.

I also know that even that environment can stagnate my creativity if I don't change it up from time to time. So we go on adventures on a whim—often. We hop in the car or matatu (a local African transport van), go somewhere we've never been before, and just see what happens. Some of our greatest memories and most creative moments have been spawned from adventures like these.

I like to scare myself a bit, just to make sure I'm still alive. That always gets the creative juice—or at least the adrenaline—flowing.

Would You Rather Be Pretty or Smart?

See if you can detect the pattern in these comments I've heard from 48 Days podcast listeners:

> "Should I do something I love or keep being a responsible provider?"
>
> "I'm torn between doing something creative or making money."
>
> "I want to be in business but feel called to be in ministry."
>
> "I know where my passions and talents are, but I don't know what God wants me to do."
>
> "I'd love to be an entrepreneur, but I'm the primary breadwinner for my family."
>
> "I'd like to help the less fortunate, but I barely have enough time for my own work."

The pattern is that all of these are artificial dichotomies. You don't have to choose one. In each case you can do *both*.

In *The 7 Habits of Highly Effective People,* Stephen Covey pointed out that most people think in terms of *either/or.*[1] If you're nice, you probably can't be firm. Or if you're confident, you are not likely to be considerate. Or if I'm buying a car from you, one of us is going to win, and one will lose. So with the false belief that life is a game of choosing, we quickly assume that we can't have two good things at once.

What if we started looking only for *and* solutions?

Look at the list above again. Is there any reason you could not do both in any of those situations? Don't deprive yourself of the use of your creativity, the desire to make money, the call to ministry, the need to be responsible, or the call to be an entrepreneur. Do it all.

Recently Joanne wanted to go to the beach, and I felt the need to stay current on my work. So who won? We both won. Why not? We went to Nokomis Beach, Florida, where I worked early each morning while Joanne basked in the sun. We typically had an early lunch, I'd work for another hour, then we'd hit the shops or be back on the beach for the gorgeous sunsets. And then we'd be at Captain Eddie's or Sharky's for dinner.[18]

Look for the *and* solutions that make your life everything you want it to be. And just for today you can have both pie and ice cream. Then live your life à la mode.

Making a Living . . . Or

How many times have you heard people say about their work, "Well, at least I'm making a living"? Maybe it would be more accurate to say, "I'm making a dying." The work they describe is unfulfilling, boring, and stressful. They dread going in on Monday morning and every other morning. Often they are embarrassed about their work and admit readily they are doing nothing meaningful, only extracting a paycheck in exchange for their time.

Does that sound like making a living? I don't think so. They may brush it off as just something we all do; work is never going to be purposeful and enjoyable. They may pretend it doesn't really matter. But then I hear painful comments like, "I feel like my soul is being sucked out of me," or "I feel like a prostitute—in exchange for my life I'm getting a paycheck."

If you're caught up in the typical American view of work, you may say you're making a living when in truth something inside you is being killed each day. Every day, millions of people rush to get to jobs they don't love, and yet those people defend their choices as responsible, practical, and realistic. How can it be responsible to live the biggest part of our lives devoid of meaning, joy, and purpose?

"Making a living" implies that you are releasing those skills and talents that make you fully alive. Doing work where the time just flies by—work that you would want to do even if you were not paid for it. Work that is meaningful, fulfilling, purposeful, and profitable.

In a recent issue of his ministry newsletter, Rick Warren, the author of *The Purpose Driven Life*, was talking about this idea of meaningful work. He referenced this verse from Ecclesiastes: "Only someone too stupid to find his way home would wear himself out with work" (10:15 GNT). How do you like that? Have you been worn out at work lately? Did you know that you've just been put in the category of being "too stupid to find your way home"?

Well, maybe that's a little harsher than it was intended to be, and you'll find softer language in other Bible translations, but I like the message. Don't be so busy trying to make a living that you're too busy to make a life.

And I don't even have space here to describe what most people are doing to themselves when they think they're making a killing. Are you making a living when you work? Is your work energizing and utilizing your best God-given talents?

Think about the times in your life when you're *most* happy. Sure, you're happy when your job is going well or if your own business is thriving. And you're happy when you have a big bank account and the stuff you want. We all know those are legitimate feelings because they're rooted in the predominantly materialistic world that's been created around us.

But I would challenge you to think about the times when you were truly happy. Those times when you were almost driven to tears because of the human connection you experienced through helping another human being or experiencing love.

The times when you've made a sacrifice to help someone or when you've averted some disaster and in the process, everyone around you was united, despite their differences.

The first blog I ever wrote was about my experience at a train station in Newark, New Jersey. There was a horrible storm that actually knocked down huge trees onto the train tracks. We huddled together in a circle to protect each other from the wind and debris. No one was more important than the next person. For just a few moments, everyone at that station became equal. It was one of the most beautiful moments I've ever experienced.

Those are the times that matter most. So why not make that your life? How can you justify knowing and understanding this dynamic yet continually going back to "reality" after the gig is over?

We create our own reality around us every day. Why not make it one full of love and life and human connection? Why do so many people view that life as something outside reality or something that other people do, like philanthropists and humanitarians?

In general, the Western priorities and governances are quite skewed. We want to make more money so we can have more happiness. So we work harder and longer. That takes more time. But we value time the most. And we want family, but they suffer most when we're always focused on money. Where does it end?

This reminds me of a brilliant story my father told me long ago.

THE MEXICAN FISHERMAN

An American businessman was at the pier of a small coastal Mexican village when a small boat with just one fisherman docked. Inside the small boat were several large yellow fin tuna. The American complimented the Mexican on the quality of his fish and asked how long it took to catch them. The Mexican replied, "Only a little while." The American then asked why he didn't stay out longer and catch more fish. The Mexican said he had enough to support his family's immediate needs.

The American then asked, "But what do you do with the rest of your time?"

The fisherman said, "I sleep late, fish a little, play with my children, take a siesta with my wife, Maria, stroll into the village each evening where I sip wine and play guitar with my amigos. I have a full and busy life."

The American scoffed, "I'm a Harvard MBA and I could help you. You should spend more time fishing and with the proceeds buy a bigger boat. With the proceeds from the bigger boat you could buy several boats; eventually you would have a fleet of fishing boats. Instead of selling your catch to a middleman you would sell directly to the processor, eventually opening your own cannery. You would control the product, processing, and distribution. You would need to leave this small coastal fishing village and move to Mexico City, then LA, and eventually NYC where you will run your expanding enterprise."

The Mexican fisherman asked, "But how long will all this take?"

To which the American replied, "Fifteen to twenty years."

"But what then?"

The American laughed and said, "That's the best part. When the time is right you would announce an IPO and sell your company stock to the public and become very rich. You would make millions."

"Millions? Then what?" the native fisherman asked.

"Then you could retire. Move to a small coastal fishing village where you would sleep late, fish a little, play with your kids, take a siesta with your wife, and stroll to the village in the evenings where you could sip wine and play your guitar with your amigos."[19]

It's a Wonderful Life—So Far

Here's another way to look at this issue. If someone saw a movie of your life so far, when the credits rolled, would he say, "Wow, that was awesome"? Or would he scratch his head and say, "I wonder what that was all about"?

Take a minute to think about your life as a movie. How does the storyline in a movie develop? There is a character who wants something and overcomes some kind of conflict to get it. If the character in the movie doesn't want something difficult to attain, there's no story. Screenwriters often use an inciting incident to begin the story. In your life an inciting incident could be a layoff, a firing, or a heart attack. These incidents occur because you're part of an exciting story. The conflicts and challenges give value and direction to your ambitions. The same principles that make a great movie also make a great life.

So you want to create memorable scenes in your movie. But remember, everything counts. Every action is a permanent part of your life story. How you talked to your spouse this morning is a scene from the movie of your life. Your behavior at lunch today will be a scene from your life.

Here are tips for making the movie of your life great:

1. Decide in advance what the story will be.
2. Welcome challenges as inciting incidents.
3. View every action as a scene in your movie.

4. Choose the other acting characters.

5. Remember that you are the director of this movie.

In 2010 my sons Kevin and Jared, my brother Nate, and I got to attend author Donald Miller's Storyline Conference in Portland, Oregon.[20] We got to write the storyline of our lives. What a great Miller boys' experience! Are you happy with the direction of your life's story—so far?

Are you aware that you are the director?

I've made a habit of creating and welcoming inciting incidents in my life. A few times per year I like to pull the rug out from under myself, just to see how I handle it.

I wrote my first blog post on December 23, 2007, during a holiday visit back to the United States. I'd been living in Rwanda for about a year and a half at that point. I was writing about why I love living in Africa and about some of those dynamics that contribute to that love. Here's a little excerpt. At the time of writing this, I had been away from Rwanda for about a month.

So much has gone on in Kigali since I've been away. Our Rwandan staff say the Sisters are doing great and even look a bit younger. I can't wait to get back and see their shining faces again. I've missed them. I've missed the children. I've missed the African life.

There is such a rawness about Africa that we don't experience here in the States. It's like those moments in life where you find yourself in some strange situation that you have never experienced or that you never imagined would happen.

I was in a horrible storm in Newark, New Jersey, one time, about eight years ago. My British friend (Ali) and I were the only white folks in the heart of the ghetto. There was no electricity anywhere in the city and it was getting dark. The wind was blowing violently, massive trees were falling down around us, huge metal trash cans were flying across the parking lot as if they were Coke cans, and a subway had derailed right in front of us. It was like nothing I could have even dreamed up.

We were all outside trying to find shelter on the side of the overcrowded subway station, which was actually closed, due to continuous vandalism. Ali and I and the rest of the adults immediately gathered up all the kids and we huddled together and protected them from the wind, rain, and debris. We were soaked and fearing for our lives. We had no shelter and the sky was ominous.

No one was thinking about skin color. No one was thinking about taking advantage of anyone. No one thought about social status or education levels or money. All of our programmed tendencies were removed instantly and we were left with only our God-given reactions. It was raw.

We protected each other. We bonded, in a matter of minutes. We embraced each other and pulled together. We served each other, just as we were created to do. Just for a moment, we were one. That is what Africa provides for me every day. I'm ready to get back to that. I'm ready to go back home [to Africa].

Over the years, I've referred to this post many times because it touches on an inciting incident that played such a vital role in making me who I am today. I've found myself craving natural disasters, power outages, and anything else that stirs things up. Why? Because these types of events tend to bring out the true humanity in all of us, for good or for bad. But those reactions are raw and human, and that's what I crave.

Those are the moments when you find out who you, and those around you, really are. Think of the times in your life when you've just survived some crazy situation or you've lost something you love or things didn't turn out the way you planned. Often, those times are some of the most defining in our lives.

Now, I don't recommend instigating disasters around you, but you can deliberately create challenging moments that bring about a similar influx of creativity and self-realization. Go to a concert you never would have gone to otherwise. Go somewhere that scares you a bit. Face a longtime fear. Go to a social event that challenges your social skills. Take on a project that really challenges your problem-solving skills.

I've always been one to jump into sink-or-swim situations because I know I'll inevitably learn something valuable about myself or whatever I'm tackling. Ultimately I'll become stronger, wiser, or more experienced, or if nothing else, I'll have a sense of accomplishment or learn a valuable lesson about how *not* to do something. Either way, it's all good.

Don't Get a Job with Benefits

After I spoke at Kent Julian's Speak It Forward Boot Camp[21], the attendees were gathered in his living room.

Chad Jeffers[22] shared an amazing short set on the dobro and then some of his personal story. Chad said years ago his dad, who is also in the music industry, told him: "If you want to make this music thing work, never get a job with benefits." The obvious implication was that if you get a job with benefits, you might become complacent and not hungry enough to follow your dream.

Wow! How many of you had a dad who told you that? More common is a dad who begged you to forget about that "music thing" and to get a job with benefits. Today Chad is a writer, speaker, and performer whose reputation has repeatedly opened doors with people like Kenny Loggins, Keith Urban, and Carrie Underwood. In fact, he has never auditioned for a position. Rather he has been told again and again, "So-and-so says, 'You're the guy'!"

Legend has it that when Cortés landed in Mexico in the 1500s, he ordered his men to burn the ships that had brought them there to remove the possibility of doing anything other than going forward into the unknown. There's something to be said about not having a safety net.

How committed are you to the success of your dream?

Is This Really Hard Work?

Don't you hear people talking about "working hard" all the time? The comment may come from a highly paid CEO, a wealthy athlete, a guy on a construction crew, or a stay-at-home mom. What gives us the feeling of working too hard?

Recently on a Saturday morning I grabbed a wheelbarrow, a shovel, and a rake and headed for the back section of a nature trail through the woods on our property. The temperature was officially at ninety-nine degrees, the wood chip pile I intended to spread was dirty and dry, and the trail wound up and down over rocks. It took me about four hours of grueling, dusty, back-breaking work to complete that section of the path. Then I went in, took a shower, and felt energized and invigorated as I joined Joanne to spend time with some friends at their lake house.

Was that hard work? In working with people in career crises for twenty years now I have observed that the work itself does not define *hard*. And the amount of pay does not correlate with the feeling of hard work. If the work allows creativity, autonomy, and a connection between effort and reward, then a sense of meaning is clear, and no one is found complaining. Conversely if there is no creativity, autonomy, or connection between effort and reward, then even the easiest work becomes hard. Don't you hear the woman at the checkout counter, having just interrupted her reading of the latest novel, complain about working so hard? But do you suppose the Beatles complained about playing eight hours a night, seven days a week, for years before we ever heard about them? No, they had the three elements of meaningful work long before they became rich as a result.

Work is a prison sentence only if it holds no meaning for you. Or as Confucius said, "Choose a job you love, and you will never have to work a day in your life."[23]

Check this out as a model for finding—or creating—your dream job.

Here's the irony about doing something that matters. Our assumption is often that if we do something humanitarian, socially responsible, or godly, we will have to subsist on what my friend Dave Ramsey calls "beans and rice." Guess what? Doing something worthwhile, something that engages your passions and your strongest talents, is likely to release more money than you could possibly eke out doing something you hate. Trust me. It's a whole lot easier to make money doing something you love than trying to be responsible or practical doing something you despise. Doing something you love will cause money to show up in unexpected ways. Just draw from your passion and your wisdom to make it happen.

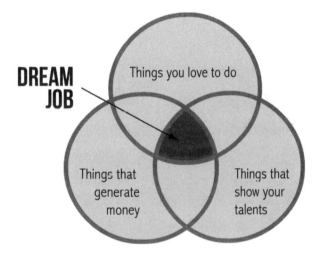

CHAPTER FIVE
Doing Work That Matters

"The Glory of God Is Man Fully Alive"

Saint Irenaeus declared in the second century: "The glory of God is man fully alive."[1] What does it mean to be fully alive in our work? How do we maximize the use of the talents God has given us?

Are you fully alive?

- Can you tell me what success means for you this year?
- Are you where you thought you'd be at this stage of your life?
- Have you ever had a sense of calling in your life? How did you hear that calling?
- Is your work a fulfillment of your life's purpose?
- Do you go home at night with a sense of meaning, peace, and accomplishment?
- If nothing changed in your life over the next five years, would that be okay?
- If you want different results next year, what are you willing to change in what you are doing now?

- Do you know the distinctions between *vocation*,
  career, and *job*?

Clarifying these questions will help you move toward being fully alive in your work.

We are seeing a dramatic shift in the workplace. No longer can one expect to graduate, get a great job, stay with that company for thirty-five years, get a gold watch, and retire. That model is gone forever. We have seen the collapse of major financial institutions, auto manufacturers, real estate companies, and thousands of smaller companies around the world. Long-standing companies like Enron, WorldCom, Tower Records, Woolworth's, Borders, and The Sharper Image simply did not survive. Others seem to be teetering on the brink of obsolescence. Powerhouse Macy's cut seven thousand jobs as people moved to online purchasing. CBS is struggling in the wake of weak print advertising dollars, and more than fifteen thousand newspaper jobs have disappeared. Blockbuster Video filed for bankruptcy protection and announced plans to close nearly one thousand stores as technology allows movie watching without the cumbersome DVD.[2]

Is anything predictable in the world of work as we have known it? Can work be more than just an exchange of time for a paycheck?

The critical question for you then is this: Can I take my unique personality, skills, and passions and blend those into meaningful, purposeful, and profitable work today? And the answer is a resounding yes, whether you are twenty-five, forty-five, or sixty-five years old.

Baby boomers assumed they would work, make lots of money, and retire in ease. Unfortunately many of them discovered that what they thought was security was simply an illusion, and the retirement they anticipated has vanished in the distance.

The next generation mistrusts the traditional work model, choosing instead to do something noble, humanitarian, or socially responsible with little thought for how that translates into income and financial stability. With changing work models the chances of having a job with guaranteed salary and benefits are diminishing. But the new models may provide *more* fulfillment, purpose, meaning, time, freedom, and flexibility. And surprisingly, many of these new innovative work models ultimately produce far more income as well.

As I mentioned in chapter 2, our work models are changing. No longer is being an employee the only option. The new work is being described by terms such as *consultants, independent contractors, contingency workers, entrepreneurs, electronic immigrants, virtual assistants,* and *freelancers.* The average length of a job in America is now 2.2 years.[3] That means that in a forty-five-year working span, a person can be expected to have eighteen to twenty different jobs. We are now told that the average length of a job for someone in his twenties is thirteen months.[4] These changes require each of us to develop a clear sense of who we are and where we are going. Otherwise we will feel victimized by those changes and feel something different from being fully alive in our work. Here's how these facts negatively affect us. According to the American Institute of Stress, a recent Gallup Poll found that

- 80 percent of workers feel stress on the job, nearly half say they need help in learning how to manage stress, and 42 percent say their coworkers need such help;
- 14 percent of respondents had felt like striking a coworker in the past year, but didn't; and
- 25 percent have felt like screaming or shouting because of job stress, and 10 percent are concerned about an individual at work they fear could become violent.[5]

Furthermore, MSN Health reports that more heart attacks occur on Monday mornings between 4:00 a.m. and 10:00 a.m. than any other six-hour period in the week,[6] and according to a December 2010 survey by job-placement firm Manpower, 84 percent of employees were planning to look for a new position in 2011. That was up from just 60 percent the previous year.[7]

The generation of 71.5 million baby boomers has seen the front edge of this volatile transition. Corporate fraud, stock market catastrophes, economic upheaval, and continuing wars around the world have eroded their sense of security and predictability. The upcoming generations no longer expect or even wish for the sameness that their parents assumed was part of growing up.

But these new generations do bring unique desires to the table. They are not just throwing out all longing for fulfilling work, economic stability, personal responsibility, and a meaningful world. In fact, they are perhaps more committed to those things than they have seen in their more materialistic parents and grandparents. According to a Harris Poll, a whopping 97 percent of Generation Y workers are looking for work that allows them "to have an impact on the world."[8] The most rapidly growing area of study in academic institutions is that of social entrepreneurship, which has been created in more than 250 colleges and universities, such as Harvard Business School, Yale School of Management, Duke, Belmont, Vanderbilt, Wharton, Oxford, and Stanford.[9]

As stated at the beginning of this chapter, Saint Irenaeus declared in the second century, "The glory of God is man fully alive." These new generations are not content to make a living—they want to be fully alive. And being fully alive implies a life that is connected to something beyond ourselves—to be part of a movement or process that will expand our individual efforts and live on after we are gone.

The wisdom of the past can blend with the passion of the

current generation in accomplishments that are socially significant, humanitarian, noble, and purposeful and yet still be personally and economically responsible.

In coaching clients through challenging career transitions, I often use this quotation from James Michener as a goal: "The master in the art of living makes little distinction between his work and his play, his labor and his leisure, his mind and his body, his information and his recreation, his love and his religion. He hardly knows which is which. He simply pursues his vision of excellence at whatever he does, leaving others to decide whether he is working or playing. To him he's always doing both."[10]

We are making the case that these goals are not mutually exclusive and that wisdom and passion are on both ends of the age continuum and can be integrated for extraordinary achievements and true success. The economic challenges of 2008–11 have served as a wake-up call for the dormant but authentic passions of the baby boomers to leave the world a better place than they found it. And the younger generations have accelerated their wisdom through access to information, technology, and travel, making them wise beyond their years. Their maturity of thought and actions in political, economic, and theological systems are bringing new light and hope to our changing world.

MORE HUMANITY, PLEASE

Prior to the 1492 invasion by Christopher Columbus and his crew, American Indians lived rather peacefully and without money. They lived communally, taking care of one another. People acted less as individuals and more as one unit.

Then we moved into the trading era, where American Indians began to trade with one another and the Europeans.

Soon society began to crave more, faster, bigger, and better. We skip ahead to the Industrial Revolution of the 1800s and 1900s. Then in 1913 Henry Ford refined the assembly line for his automobiles, and production methods leapt forward once again.

The growing demand for mass production created a dynamic whereby society turned a blind eye to sweatshop labor and slavery. We've seen this evolution time and time again throughout history.

The fair trade movement began in Europe in the 1960s as a movement toward more ethical production methods. In 1989 the World Fair Trade Organization was launched, solidifying a worldwide movement. It became sort of an international minimum wage standard. Certainly a step in the right direction.

The Internet has fostered transparency like we've never seen. The veil has been lifted, and the movement toward higher standards for ethics and ecologically sound production methods is growing exponentially. There is certainly nothing that would indicate that society would ever allow for a movement back in the other direction.

In short, we went from taking care of one another (essentially for free), to trading, to mass production, to sweatshops and slavery (again), and finally to a more pervasive expectation of ethical and eco-friendly production standards (fair trade).

I believe the next progression will be toward a more personal connection between the consumer and the producer of the goods. When it comes to art and creativity, there is no substitute for humanity.

If we're producing technological devices, for sure, let the robots do that. But when it comes to artful creations such as fashion, painting, sculpting, and music, we want as much humanity infused as possible.

There was a time when society wanted everyone to have the same cool purse or shirt. Now we want to be individuals. We want something unique that expresses our individuality, with a human touch. The closer we can get to the producer, the better. We want to know the story of the hands that created what we're wearing. Where did they come from? What inspired them? What life experience compelled them to design this way? Why did they use these materials?

As an ethical fashion label, we at KEZA know that the more we can connect someone to the artisan who created the product, the higher the perceived value of the product. The more value we give to the human story behind a product, the more that dynamic will be fostered by the masses.[11]

In an age of the rise of the machines, this is certainly a trend we can get behind and one that is here to stay.

Just after writing this, I discovered a brilliant organization called IOWEYOU. It exemplifies the concept I just described.[12]

No Passion: There's a Hole in Your Bucket

What are you passionate about?

Too frequently I hear in response to that question: "Nothing," or "I really don't know."

Certainly you've met people who have a clear passion. They can't wait to get up in the morning and start on their work. They are eager and enthusiastic, and they understand their purpose and are committed to living it out. That kind of passion comes from knowing what you were born to do. Follow me around for a day or two and then decide whether I'm passionate about my work.

Passion helps you get more done in less time. It helps you make better decisions with less stress and indecision. When you know your passion and have work that expresses that passion, you become a magnet for others—people who are willing to hitch their wagon to your enthusiasm. You will become a lightning rod for not only your efforts, but you will focus the talents and abilities of those around you, and your work will be magnified with little effort. People want to be connected to something big—something that will make a difference.

Working on your own without passion is exhausting. Your best efforts cannot stop the slow drain of energy and life. You don't get the strength of those around you; you have a big leak in your own bucket.

Do you have a passion that's contagious?

Give Me an $80,000 Salary, and I'll Catch Lunch

I read in our local paper that a high school senior, right here in my hometown of Franklin, Tennessee, received a fishing scholarship to attend Bethel University in McKenzie, Tennessee. The fishing team coach, Garry Mason, says they wanted to be the first college in America to offer fishing scholarships. He is willing to have young women on the team as well.[13]

On what appears to be a related note, Collegegrad.com reports that 80 percent of 2009 college graduates moved back in with their parents upon graduating—most without jobs of any kind. "Many factors are responsible for the trend of recent graduates moving back in with their parents," said Adeola Ogunwole, Collegegrad.com director of marketing and PR. "The economy is tough right now. Every year, living independently becomes more expensive and entry level jobs become more competitive."

Another factor, said Ogunwole, is that Gen Y students—born in the 1980s and 1990s—tend to have close ties with their parents, depend on them for support and guidance, and feel no stigma at moving back home after graduation.[14]

Perhaps it's also due to the marketability of the degrees being granted. Just what does one do with a degree in history, philosophy, or religion? And if you're looking for a grant to help with even more obscure areas of study, check these out:

- The Sammy Award: $7,500 is awarded to students who demonstrate academic success and leadership skills and can wear a milk moustache.[15]
- Chick and Sophie Major Memorial Duck Calling Contest: $1,500 is awarded to the student who can call ducks with the most flair.[16]

"Many recent graduates are turning down good job offers, holding out for better jobs and salaries in the belief that a college degree entitles them to more than entry level," stated Ogunwole.

I'm Back with My Parents—and Stuck!

Here's a question sent in from a 48 Days podcast listener:

> Dan, I recently lost my teaching job and had to move back home with my parents, not exactly what I had in the plans at thirty. My biggest fear at this point is that I have been living without a sense of purpose for a few years now. I have a lot of passion and determination, but have no clue what God created me to do. HELP!!!

And here's my response: I agree that moving back home with your parents at age thirty was probably not your dream of success. We all have times of reevaluation, so see this as one of those times. But the real concern here is your statement that "I have been living without a sense of purpose for a few years now." Losing a job or living with your parents is a small detail to be addressed compared to not having a sense of purpose. It's impossible to present yourself with enthusiasm and confidence if all you're trying to do is get a job.

But at thirty you have enough life experience to look back and see clear patterns:

- What are your unique skills and abilities?
- What are your personality traits?
- What are those recurring dreams and passions?

In just observing and clarifying these characteristics you will be able to see patterns form. And it's simply in the blending of these that you define your purpose (or you may refer to it as *calling, mission,* or *destiny*). You cannot expect success to show up or to have any sustained passion without knowing your purpose.

Go to 48Days.com and click on Resources.[17] You'll see worksheets. Find the form for helping you create your personal mission statement. Spend two hours working through the steps to have clarification of your purpose and a plan of action. You'll get on track, move out of your parents' house, and move on with your life. Being a boomerang kid is fine for a while, but now it's time to fly on your own.

But Isn't Work Just a Curse from God?

What we do for a living, in a ministry, or in our family life is the application of our calling. Apart from engaging our creativity, artistry, skills, abilities, and gifts, it is impossible to live out our calling. We cannot complete God's call in a vacuum. We must be engaged in work of some kind. We are all called to a life of service and ministry; the way we are equipped to do that varies from person to person.

But if we view work as a curse, how does that have an impact on our effectiveness? How can we be salt and light[18] if the biggest use of our time is in something we dread? Can we really draw others to faith if we are miserable in how we choose to work?

Yes, I know. Genesis 3:17–19 records God's words to Adam: "I have placed a curse upon the soil. All your life you will struggle to extract a living from it. It will grow thorns and thistles for you, and you shall eat its grasses. All your life you will sweat to master it, until your dying day." And some have hung on to that passage, claiming that all work is a curse from God.

Does that really mean that any work we have to do today is part of that curse?

- If the only reason you work is to get a paycheck, you probably see work as a curse.

- If you dread Monday mornings, you probably see work as a curse.
- If you don't get along with your boss, you probably see work as a curse.
- If your work doesn't use your best talents, you probably see work as a curse.
- If your work leaves you drained and exhausted, you probably see work as a curse.
- If going to work makes you anxious or fearful, you probably see work as a curse.
- If you're worried about getting fired, you probably see work as a curse.

How can we engage in work but not view it as a curse? What is a godly perspective of work? Adam moved out of God's will. Thus by the sweat of his brow he would have to work. Anxiety, frustration, discouragement, and anger bring sweat to our brows. When there is an authentic alignment of our best talents with our work, we don't sweat. Rather, we enjoy the process of work that is fulfilling, purposeful, and profitable.

And if we read on in Genesis—just five more chapters—we will find some new and exciting information. God had enough of dealing with those early people with their evil ways and decided to wipe the face of the earth clean and start again with just Noah and his family. Then came the Flood. No, the one before Steve Carell in *Evan Almighty*. After that original flood, Noah had a nice party that made God pretty happy with the way things were going. And God said, "I will never do it again—I will never again curse the earth, destroying all living things, even though man's bent is always toward evil from his earliest youth, and even though he does such wicked things. As long as the earth remains, there will be springtime and harvest, cold and heat, winter and summer, day and night" (Gen. 8:21–22).

So the curse has been lifted. It was there for only five short chapters in the entire Bible and certainly is no longer in place for us. Work is to be enjoyed, to be a release of the very best we have to offer, and to be used as our greatest tool for living out our godly callings.

Even in his most pessimistic moments, Solomon said "that every man should eat and drink, and enjoy the good of all his labour, it is the gift of God" (Eccl. 3:13 KJV).

And Paul wrote, "Servants, do what you're told by your earthly masters. And don't just do the minimum that will get you by. Do your best. Work from the heart for your real Master, for God, confident that you'll get paid in full when you come into your inheritance. Keep in mind always that the ultimate Master you're serving is Christ. The sullen servant who does shoddy work will be held responsible. Being a follower of Jesus doesn't cover up bad work" (Col. 3:22–25 MSG).

MY BEST IS WHAT MATTERS

Fortunately I was raised to see work as a gift. What else could I do on this earth that would provide me with such applicable wisdom, knowledge, understanding, and fulfillment than doing my best? And it's not about your output; it's about the discoveries you make and the relationships you create along the way. It's also about the experience and satisfaction that come from knowing you've done your best.

My brother and I raced BMX bikes for all of our childhood and then road bikes after that. Racing was a way of life for our family, and we all loved it. It was a real-life experience, and we didn't get depressed when we lost. It wasn't about winning. It was about doing our best. Every time we lost, it was just another installment in a much bigger game of figuring out who we were and how we could hone the skills that contributed to being our best.

My parents didn't scorn us for losing—ever. If I lost, Dad would ask, "Did you do your best?" If the answer was yes, all was well. If the answer was no, it became quite clear which battle I truly lost. It wasn't the race against other riders; it was me losing the opportunity to gain the fulfillment of knowing I did my best, and that was a true loss.

I am always looking for creative projects to give to Francois so he can practice doing his best and ultimately experience that fulfillment. I talk to him a lot about the difference between doing a good job and doing his best. Anyone can do a good job if the paycheck depends on it. But doing something extraordinary has a much better payoff than just a paycheck.

I've always been able to lay my head on my pillow with peace in my mind, knowing I've done my best. That peace has never been dependent on whether or not I failed, succeeded, or took too long to finish. It has always been solely dependent on whether or not I know that I did my absolute best.

My best has always been a result of dedication, study, research, apprenticing, practicing, diligence, and sowing passion and love into everything I do. If I've done that, I am at peace with whatever the results are. I don't get caught up in the results. It's the journey that is important. If I am dedicated to always giving my best during the journey, I've already set the stage for achieving the best results. And if I fail, it's just another investment in the journey.

This view has always given me a healthy work ethic and understanding of the purpose and potential of doing extraordinary work. Mistakes happen. Failure happens. But no one can take my best from me. That's mine. And that's where I get peace.

Do these words of Kahlil Gibran describe your work?

Work is love made visible.

And if you cannot work with love but only with distaste, it is better that you should leave your work and sit at the gate of the temple and take alms of those who work with joy.

For if you bake bread with indifference, you bake a bitter bread that feeds but half man's hunger.

And if you grudge the crushing of the grapes, your grudge distils [sic] a poison in the wine.

And if you sing though as angels, and love not the singing, you muffle man's ears to the voices of the day and the voices of the night.[19]

Is your work love made visible?

You're Never Uncalled

I don't need to add much to this. As jobs or businesses come and go, be reminded that your calling remains constant. And that calling is always going to be evidenced in work that makes you fully alive.

We may at times be unemployed, but
no one ever becomes uncalled.
—OS GUINNESS[20]

What's That in Your Hand?

Remember when God spoke to Moses at the burning bush? God told Moses he wanted him to go back to Egypt and lead the people out to the promised land. Moses looked around and said, "You've got to be kidding. I'm not the person for a job like that." God assured Moses he would prepare the way and he would provide some pretty convincing miracles. Still Moses had a hard time believing he was up to the task. He pleaded, "I can't speak well, I don't have a college degree, and I'm a convicted felon. Please, send anyone else!"

Now here we have someone with an obvious opportunity. Wouldn't you like for God to lay out such a clear plan for you and to promise success in advance? But that wasn't good enough for Moses. He kept trying to convince God that he didn't have any of the necessary requirements for accomplishing this big job. Moses said, "They won't believe me. I don't have anything to qualify me for doing something great." God said, "What is that in your hand?" If you don't remember, it was his shepherd's staff, which turned out to be a pretty significant part of his leadership. He parted the Red Sea with it and did some other pretty cool stuff. (You can read the whoe story in Exodus 3–4.)

If you think you're stuck, don't have any unusual talents, don't have the right degrees, and don't have the credibility to have people take you seriously, let me ask you a question: "What do you have in your hand?" What natural talents do you have? What is it you do with excellence? Do you make beautiful candles? Delicious bread? Encourage the elderly? Grow stunning flowers? Handle your children with grace? You get the idea. Just look at what you have right in front of you.

With God's help you may already have everything you need for greatness. Don't balk when you hear your call.

Our work is evidence of our faith. Saint Benedict once said, *"Orare est laborare, laborare est orare,"* which means "to pray is to work, to work is to pray."[21] Work connects my spirit to God's. In the perfect world God created, Adam and Eve were given the opportunity to tend and care for the garden. Sounds rather like work to me. That was a privilege—the application of the perfect life and their highest calling. That's what it means to be fully alive.

CHAPTER SIX

Who Are You, and Why Are You Here?

There is an old story about Akiva, the rabbi, who had been in the village to gather some supplies. Walking back to his cottage, he absentmindedly took the wrong path. Suddenly a voice came through the darkness: "Who are you, and why are you here?"

Shocked to awareness, Akiva realized he had wandered into the Roman garrison, and the voice had come from the young sentry keeping guard. But being a rabbi, he answered the question with another question. "How much do they pay you to stand guard and ask that question of all who approach?"

The sentry, now seeing that this was not an intruder but a rabbi, answered meekly, "Five drachmas a week, sir."

At that point the rabbi offered, "Young man, I will double your pay if you come with me, stand in front of my cottage, and ask me that question each morning as I begin my day: Who are you, and why are you here?"

As baby boomers are confronted with economic volatility and the younger generations are looking for direction, both groups are asking themselves this question: "Who are you, and why are you here?" Terms like *mission, purpose, destiny,* and *calling* are the concepts driving clarity in work and life.

Without clarity on who I am and why I am here, anything becomes a possibility. If I approach each day with no vision, I will respond based on the squeaky wheel principle—anything that pops will redirect my attention. Brian Tracy says, "If you don't set goals for yourself, you are doomed to work to achieve the goals of someone else."[1] Having a clear mission statement for my life allows me to decide in advance the life I want to live.[2] A mission statement identifies my reason for existing. It creates a focus for every activity in my life. And it needs to be specific enough that I can weigh any activity. It's a clarifying process to eliminate meaningless activity. Sometimes I see people create a mission statement that sounds great but means little. It's so generic it would fit anyone who breathes. Here's one: "I want to love God and serve him forever." I know that sounds all warm and fuzzy, but I have no idea what that person is going to do tomorrow morning when he gets up, and I'm pretty confident he doesn't either. Thus you can have a very positive and even godly sounding mission statement that is essentially meaningless in shaping your daily activities.

I don't know any high achievers who get up in the morning and just kind of see what happens—just do whatever seems important at the time. No, people who accomplish things decide in advance how they will invest their time. They have a plan. That's what a mission statement does. It helps you decide before the week begins what activities line up with your values and priorities.

Having clear goals and a mission statement is much like having a budget. If I know I have $168 coming in, I can decide in advance exactly how I will spend that money. In the same way, I also know that I will have 168 hours in the coming week. I can decide now how to invest those precious hours so I spend them doing things that matter.

It has been said that indecision is the greatest thief of opportunity. If I have no goals and no clear direction, any idea that comes my way could be a reasonable option. So that means if I come up with five ideas, I may start evaluating all five. Weeks and months may pass, and I still have not come to a decision to narrow the choices and take action. I can easily get trapped in the studying, analyzing, and researching phase with no productive action taken. Having clear goals and a mission statement allows me to look at those five ideas and immediately decide what embraces my predetermined goals and what does not. Even good ideas need to be eliminated so I can focus my activities to take me to higher levels of success.

A couple years ago I was presented with an opportunity that would have given me massive national exposure. The financial projections were astronomical. But this opportunity would have required me to travel about half the time. I did some brief research before turning it down. I didn't even consult with other advisers before making that decision. Having a clear mission statement allowed me to instantly recognize the conflict with personal values that would have been required. That's the power of clarity regarding "Who am I, and why am I here?"

Stop Doing That

If there's one reason I hear more than any other for failed New Year's resolutions, it's "I just didn't have the time." Often success in goals comes not by adding more to our busy lives, but by deciding what we're going to stop doing. When I stopped serving on boards and  going to civic and committee meetings, I freed up significant time that I now spend writing, which I consider my number one priority.

What can you stop doing to accomplish your goals?

Don't say you don't have enough time. You have exactly the same number of hours per day that were given to Helen Keller, Pasteur, Michelangelo, Mother Teresa, Leonardo da Vinci, Thomas Jefferson, and Albert Einstein.

—H. JACKSON BROWN JR.³

Inventive Success

Thomas Alva Edison's life was filled with purpose. When he spoke about his success, he said,

The most important factors of invention can be described in a few words.

1. They must consist of definite knowledge as to what one wishes to achieve.

2. One must fix his mind on that purpose with persistence and begin searching for that which he seeks, making use of all the accumulated knowledge of the subject which he has or can acquire from others.

3. He must keep on searching, no matter how many times he may meet with disappointment.

4. He must refuse to be influenced by the fact that somebody else may have tried the same idea without success.

5. He must keep himself sold on the idea that the solution of his problem exists somewhere and that he will find it.⁴

Are You More Than What You Have Become?

Remember the scene in *The Lion King* where Simba is being challenged to go back home and be the king he was born to be? Simba ran from his destiny; the struggle in confronting his mean uncle was just too difficult. But in that memorable scene he looks in the water and sees the subtle reflection of his father, Mufasa, who says, "You have forgotten who you are. . . . Look inside yourself, Simba. You are more than what you have become. . . . Remember who you are."[5]

Be clear about what is being said here. Mufasa didn't tell Simba he should have gotten another degree, should be living in a bigger house, or should be making more money. He simply said, "You are more than what you have become." *Becoming* more is much different than having or doing more.

It's easier to quantify *doing* than *being*.

We can quantify what we do: how many sales we made, how many miles we drove, how many chairs we built, or how many pages we wrote. It's also easy to see things that need to be done: dishes that need to be washed, beds that need to be made, or podcasts that need to be recorded. *Being* is harder to quantify and measure: being a great mom, a spiritual leader, a compassionate friend, an understanding boss, or a caring, loving neighbor.

Becoming more may require *doing* less.

Are you destined to be more than you have become?

When people close to death are questioned about anything they would do differently, one common theme rises to the top: "I wish I'd had the courage to live a life true to myself, not the life others expected of me."[6] This is the most common regret of all.

When someone realizes his life is almost over, it's easy to look back and see how many dreams have gone unfulfilled. That realization helps to explain much of the angst and frustration we are seeing in retirement centers and nursing homes. It's critically important to honor your dreams along the way. When you are on your deathbed, the opinions of others fade alongside the recognition that you have not lived an authentic life. My work with those making midlife corrections in their careers is largely that of simply peeling back the layers of others' expectations to reveal once again those clear and passionate childhood dreams. In those we discover work that is meaningful, purposeful, and profitable.

Life offers many choices. It is *your* life. Choose consciously, choose wisely, seek godly counsel, but choose honestly.

Horse Head or *Mona Lisa*

When I was thirteen years old, I painted a horse head with a paint-by-numbers layout. I thought it was pretty good, but now that I've seen some real masterpieces I realize it was pretty amateurish. The paint was clumpy where I tried to stay inside the identified lines. It didn't look real; it just looked like I did a good job of painting. My wife, Joanne, on the other hand, has drawn some amazing pieces—always starting with a blank canvas and then allowing her imagination to direct her brush or pencil.

I realize now that life's opportunities are presented to us in much the same way. If we paint by the numbers (take the first job, put money in CDs, buy a Ford car, purchase shirts at JCPenney, and have two weeks' vacation every year), we will see predictable results. You know what it's going to be—and it might be good—but it will never be amazing to you or anyone else. The only way to get a masterpiece is to start with a blank canvas. Of course, with a blank canvas you could also end up with a disaster that you decide to throw away. But the very next one may be the masterpiece that will make the world remember you.

While you may think that this is about willingness to take risk or that it's a reflection of personality style, I think it's more about dreaming, imagining, and taking action. And this is not just a business or career question; it's more a question of the kinds of lives we want to live. Think of Mother Teresa, Nelson Mandela, Bono, Oprah, Rick Warren, Howard Schultz, or Billy Graham. Their personality styles cover the entire range of possibilities, and we would not consider them risk takers in the sense of bungee jumping or hang gliding. But all of them had big dreams, started with a blank canvas, and then took action to create their unique masterpieces.

Here's a synopsis of the principles involved in moving from a blank canvas to something meaningful. Success is never an accident. It typically starts as imagination, becomes a dream, stimulates a goal, and grows into a plan of action—which then inevitably meets with opportunity. Don't get stuck along the way.

So you get to choose what you are creating today—a horse head or the *Mona Lisa*.

I'm Boring. Can I Get Ahead Anyway?

Here are two related questions from 48 Days podcast listeners.[7] The first one asks,

Dan, I was non-renewed from my teaching job last spring and have been applying to jobs for eight months now, with no luck. I have had around ten interviews. In the last interview, the principal told me that out of fifty-eight applicants, they interviewed only seven, and of the seven, I was one of the top four. When I asked what I could have done better, he said, "Be more animated." I have been given the same feedback from my old principal and a few other people. I have tried smiling more, using more intonation in my voice, and saying things like, "One thing I love about teaching is . . ." I am worried that I am not being hired because of my perceived lack of enthusiasm, even though I love teaching. Do you have any tips on how to be more animated?

And the second asks,

I have recently changed jobs. I sincerely want to do well, learn all I can, and get along with people. However, I am sure I come across as quite boring to others. . . . How can an introvert get ahead in the fast-paced business environment?

Here are some quick tips to make yourself a more attractive candidate in any situation:

- Listen to your own voice. Do you sound enthusiastic?
- Look someone directly in the eyes. Shifting eyes tell the person that you are not really interested and are low in self-confidence.
- Smile more, even when you are talking.
- Practice a firm handshake.
- Sit up straight, and hold your shoulders back.
- Listen carefully when someone is talking to you.
- Walk 25 percent faster than you normally would.
- Let go of resentment, unforgiveness, and guilt.
- Express gratitude for everything in your life.

Do those things, and people will want you on their team. Nothing here requires time, money, or an additional degree. You can start today and have new opportunities show up immediately.

When you become a person other people want to be around, you open yourself up to new opportunities as well. Try it and see.

Don't I Just Wait on God?

I hear a lot of people explaining long periods of inactivity as "waiting on God." As a coach, I cringe, wanting to tell them they aren't going to get any points on the board if they aren't even in the game.

In crises it's easy to shift responsibility—and blame—to God. Certainly we know he is all-powerful. But what does that mean in regard to what is expected of me? Can I expect God to literally pay my rent, find a job for me, or deal with the bank's demands? At some point we become God's hands and feet. Without us his work does not get done. And his work is not just preaching, praying, or proselytizing. It's mowing yards, making violins, building houses, delivering pizzas, or teaching schoolkids—with excellence.

> Past the seeker as he prayed came the crippled and the beggar and the beaten. And seeing them . . . he cried, "Great God, how is it that a loving creator can see such things and yet do nothing about them?" . . . God said, "I did do something. I made you."
>
> **—AUTHOR UNKNOWN**[8]

Evangelist Hudson Taylor once said, "I used to ask God to help me. Then I asked if I might help Him. I ended up asking him to do His work through me."[9] Knowing our unique talents is critical to completing our purpose and calling. Then we can be engaged in meaningful and fulfilling work. Periods of reflection and meditation can be helpful for clarification and confirmation, but then we must take action.

Here's more on this same theme.

Pray with Your Legs

Frederick Douglass once said, "I prayed for twenty years but received no answer until I prayed with my legs."[10] I referenced this quotation once, and it prompted a whole lot of questions from my readers. People wanted to know what it means, and furthermore, they wanted to know of scripture that supports whatever it means.

Yes, I see far too many people who are praying for solutions and answers and simply living in that prayerful mode—hands folded and eyes closed, waiting on God to supernaturally give them the specific answers that will remove their challenges. So just how does God answer our prayers?

Imagine any of these situations with me:

- You really need a job.
- You'd like a better car.
- You want to make peace with your spouse.
- Your lawn mower is broken.
- You want to have a best-selling book.
- You would like to have a college degree.
- You want to be a more effective parent.
- You must have $5,000 for a new air-conditioning unit.

I believe God is the providential supplier of everything we need. But I also believe that his delivery system requires our active participation—praying with our legs. If you need a job, identify thirty to forty target companies, contact each of them three times, and God will provide a job. If you want a best-selling book, write something of value, be willing to persist through the rejection of fourteen publishers as Max Lucado did with his first book (his books have now sold more than thirty million copies)—and watch God open doors. If you want a college degree, explore six options for doing so that are possible even while you continue working. Block out two hours a day for focused study, and see God allow that degree to be yours.

Can I find scripture to support faith and prayer that involves our legs? Oh, yeah. My favorite is Exodus 14:15. Moses was dealing with those whining, complaining children of Israel who saw the Egyptians coming after them in the desert. I can just see them on their knees, praying and begging God to solve their problems. The verse states, "The Lord said to Moses, 'Quit praying and get the people moving! Forward, march!'"

God provides food for the birds, but he doesn't just show up and throw it in their nest. Sometimes the exercise of faith we need most may be to engage our spiritual quadriceps, stretch those hamstrings, and use our glutei maximi for something other than supporting our bodies while we pray.

Burn Those Self-Help Books

Here's a podcast listener's question:

> Dan, you mentioned Wattles' book, *The Science of Getting Rich.*[11] I have heard strong negative reaction to such books (*Think and Grow Rich*, specifically)[12] among believers. (And my wife is among them, unfortunately.) What is your response to Christians who are antagonistic toward those books? How can I persuade my wife to consider their message?

Here is how I replied. The issue is this: How much initiative do we take in our own lives as opposed to just letting God direct our every move? I've never seen God show up at the bank to make my mortgage payment or to pay the lawn guys for mowing my grass. Just recently I was driving Joanne's car and noticed it was low on gas. It was raining like crazy—I pulled into the gas station—man, I would have loved it if God had just showed up and pumped gas for me. But no, like always, I had to get out in the rain, pump the gas myself, and pull money out of my pocket to pay for it.

Do I think that we're just all on our own? Certainly not. How then does God help or equip us? Last year we had a private concert here in the sanctuary on our property in Franklin, Tennessee, with Ted Yoder, the 2010 National Hammered Dulcimer Champion.[13] Ted told me that in the early years people always told him he was so gifted, and he often wondered why God hadn't made him successful. But then he discovered being gifted means there was the seed of a talent, and that seed needed to be nurtured by hours and hours of practice, asking for opportunities to play, scraping enough money together to produce that first album, and developing that seed into a national championship. Seeds of any kind typically require fertilizer, water, and hard work before they grow into a profitable and appealing plant.

Have you ever noticed that even if God allows you to have a dream, you're expected to work to make it happen? If you're chosen for the football team at your school, then you have to practice and work out hard, day after day, to keep your place. If you're accepted into a prestigious college, you have to study to keep your grades up, or that college will ask you to leave. It seems that even when dreams are coming true, God requires our part in the process.

There is a spiritual life lesson for all of us to gain from seeing what happened in Ted Yoder's success. Yes, we can have dreams, and yes, those dreams may come into view, but it requires a clear plan of action on our part. It requires imagination. It requires desire, hard work, self-discipline, and faith.

The life I have today was not merely God's gift to Joanne and me. The land we live on, the degrees attained, the books written, and the friendships established are the results of God's creation having been shaped and molded by human intelligence and hard work. An ancient prayer describes how this works:

> Blessed are you, Lord, God of all creation.
> Through your goodness we have this bread to offer,
> which earth has given and human hands have made.
> It will become for us the bread of life.
> Blessed be God for ever.[14]

That prayer reveals a profound spiritual principle: God's gifts are raw materials, not finished products. Think about the most revered sacrament in the church—Holy Communion. Does God give us bread and wine? Where can you find those in nature? You can't. God makes wheat; he doesn't make bread. He makes grapes, not wine. But when we take the raw materials God gives us, we can add our work and give them back to him as an offering.

I remember reading in the most popular self-help book available: "Even when we were with you, we commanded you this: If anyone will not work, neither shall he eat" (2 Thess. 3:10 NKJV).

This is a picture of the spiritual life for each of us. Every one of us has special gifts: singing, writing, gardening, painting, drawing, programming a computer, selling products, teaching others, or encouraging others. Whatever our gift, it's a raw product. It has limited value until we apply the discipline necessary to make it useful to ourselves and others.

We get nothing but rough materials. God doesn't hand us the finished product. Life may even bring us obstacles or heartache along the way. But ultimately our lives are the bread that we prepare. Our lives are what those around us see as the result of what we've done with those raw materials.

The issue is balance. Is it all us? No! Is it all God? No! We develop something great from the raw products God has given us. The debate about books like *The Science of Getting Rich* or *Think and Grow Rich* comes from people who resist personal responsibility in developing the seeds of talent God has given them.

I enjoy the writings of Franciscan priest Richard Rohr. He comments on how to joyfully surrender ourselves to God and how to pray: "Asking for something from God does not mean talking God into it; it means an awakening of the gift within ourselves."[15]

Drunk on the Job but in Church Every Sunday

Here's a question that, like many of my readers, you may have: "Dan, what kind of a role do you see faith or spirituality playing in having a fruitful, rewarding career?"

I think we often create an artificial dichotomy in which we divide what is *spiritual* and what is *secular*. I think if we are spiritual beings, everything in our lives is spiritual. I'm not a person of faith for fifty-eight minutes on Sunday morning and then just a worker bee the rest of the week. My work ought to be an expression of my faith. And trust me, what I'm doing on Thursday morning tells people more about what I believe and value than looking at the back of my head for a few minutes on Sunday.

Our work is our best opportunity to live out our calling. It's where we should get a sense of peace, accomplishment, and joy. And it's definitely our greatest opportunity for true ministry. We should accept the challenge to use our strongest skills and talents in our daily work. We will experience the sweet spot we all crave, and we will find financial rewards that show up in unexpected ways.

In a 1942 essay titled "Why Work?" Dorothy Sayers wrote,

> How can any one remain interested in a religion which seems to have no concern with nine-tenths of his life? The Church's approach to an intelligent carpenter is usually confined to exhorting him not to be drunk and disorderly in his leisure hours, and to come to church on Sundays. What the Church should be telling him is this: that the very first demand that his religion makes upon him is that he should make good tables.[16]

So are you making good tables or just collecting a paycheck?

Chicken Manure and Life Direction

I feel bad for kids today who come out of college without ever having had a job. Those first jobs are a great way to experience the real world and clarify your true talents.

I sold Christmas cards, peddled sweet corn out of a little trailer, cleaned fence rows, shoveled chicken waste, bought and sold bicycles, waxed cars, and grew popcorn before I was sixteen years old. By the time I got to college, I knew I wanted to use my brains more than my muscles.

Here are just a few jobs held by people whom you may know for other vocations today:

- As a teenager Mick Jagger worked as an ice-cream salesman. After entering the London School of Economics, he also worked as a porter at a mental hospital.[17]

- Need a rat catcher? Call Warren Beatty. He caught rodents to pay the bills before hitting it big.[18]
- Warren Buffett's first job was at his grandfather's grocery store, although he eventually worked his way up to a gig at JCPenney.[19]
- Before rising to prominence with Black Sabbath, Ozzy Osbourne worked in a slaughterhouse.[20]
- As a young man, Matthew McConaughey wanted to get away from Texas for a while, so he spent a year in Australia. To support himself, he took on a number of jobs, including one that involved shoveling chicken manure.[21]
- Jimmy Stewart was a man of many talents, from acting to being an Army Air Corps colonel. As a young man, though, he had a job painting the lines on roads, and he spent two summers as a magician's assistant.[22]
- Bill Cosby played four sports in high school, but he still found time to sell produce, shine shoes, and work as a stock boy at a supermarket.[23]
- Tom Cruise's family moved around a lot when he was young, but during one stint in Louisville he picked up extra cash as a paperboy.[24]

Most early jobs are not a mistake or misdirection; they are simply part of the clarification process. But if young people are "privileged" enough not to have to work, they often end up with a fine education and lives that are off track. Or they discover at age forty-five that they are living someone else's dream.

When my kids were young, we allowed them to work for the money they wanted for movies, cars, and goodies. I was confident that what they were becoming was more important than what they were doing.

My Life Is a Mess

What do you tell people when you first meet them? Like anyone else, I can tell my life story as a healthy version or a victim version.

I grew up in a home where we didn't even have running water until I was in the eighth grade. I knew nothing but poverty. As a five-year-old, I was forced to get up at 5:30 a.m. to do my share of the farming chores. Most Christmases I got a new pair of blue jeans—my one pair for the coming year. I was not allowed to wear neckties or fancy clothes. Because of my parents' legalistic religious beliefs, I was not allowed to go to movies, dances, or sporting events. Our home was rigid and somber with little laughter. I received zero financial help for college from my parents. I hated the cold weather in Ohio. If only I had been born into a family with more opportunity.

Or . . .

In my family we learned how to make good use of everything; nothing was wasted. We grew our own food, and I created toys from things other families discarded. As a small boy I had the opportunity to experience real work and to begin my commitment to work that was meaningful and profitable. With no TV or radio in our house I became an avid reader, and that opened me up to a wealth of wisdom and knowledge that serves me well today. I worked right through my college years and valued the education I was paying for myself. My father's devotion to his religious views prompted me to study deeply and formulate beliefs to which I could be equally committed. Today I value the work ethic and the uncompromising integrity I learned in that strict Amish/Mennonite environment. As my own man I wore neckties until I came to my realization that there was more than legalism to provide reason for not wearing the silly things. The creativity and ingenuity I experienced as a child served me in a thousand ways in helping me see opportunities that others miss.

Both versions of my life are equally true. If you'd just met me, which of those stories would make you want to get to know me more? Which one do you think makes me more confident and happier and gives me more energy today?

What is your story? Even if you lost your job, your dog died, you've got heartburn, and they repossessed the truck, what story do you want to be replaying in your mind to move to a higher level of success? What picture are you presenting to others? If you're telling yourself an unhealthy story of your life, it will perpetuate the same reality. Creating a healthy story could change the way you see your life and the way others see and respond to you.

Oh, yeah. That's me in the white shirt in the picture; I probably had a homemade slingshot in my pocket.

THE WORLDVIEW SPACE

After years of living in East Africa, I understand more than ever the power of a balanced perspective. When I operate from this perspective, I incorporate much more of humanity into my decisions, as opposed to just my particular needs or desires.

Our perspective directly affects our attitude and, more specifically, our default settings. It's easy to foster a habit of believing our individual circumstances are devastating or incapacitating. But when something goes wrong and we default to a worldview perspective, life seems a lot more manageable.

Remember the times when your perspective has been rocked because you heard of someone less fortunate overcoming outrageous circumstances? How did that affect your perspective? You likely had a moment when you realized your situation really wasn't that bad in comparison. And maybe you felt a little more grateful for what you have and a little less wanting for what you don't.

The same principle applies to our perspective of our experiences. We can view them as negative and debilitating, or we can recognize the valuable lessons we learned along the way. It's easy to weigh ourselves down with self-pity and negativity when our little bubble of life is in jeopardy. But when you take a moment to stick your head out of the bubble and account for what's really going on from a big picture perspective, life doesn't seem so rough after all.

Your perspective is a choice, and it plays a pivotal role in the reality you create around you. It certainly deserves deliberate attention. Something beautiful happens during the transition from a myopic, self-focused perspective to one that incorporates a broader, more encompassing perspective. When you're experiencing difficulties, pull your head up and take all the factors, not just the little negativity at hand, into account. Then see if everything still seems so bad. Sometimes you'll recognize a diamond in the rough rather than a reason to call it quits. I call this the *worldview space.*

What if you lived in that space? What if it were your default setting? What if anytime something bad happened, you automatically took the big picture into consideration?

When I'm faced with an extremely difficult situation, I reflect on the many others who suffer so much more than I could ever fathom. It's the difference between feeling devastated and realizing the problem I'm facing is not so insurmountable after all. What can I gain from this? How can I turn this into a positive?

Living in the worldview space prevents difficult circumstances from controlling your outlook on life. It empowers you to quickly and methodically overcome sadness, self-doubt, relationship issues, and just about anything else that would get you down. Your attitude toward life should be deliberate, not circumstantial.

How to Disable Your Kids

A Chinese university has set up a dormitory for overprotective parents. The University in Wuhan, in Hubei province, now has so many anxious parents hanging around the university that authorities have been forced to convert the sports hall to allow them to sleep on the floor.

A university spokesman said, "They often can't accept that

their children have now left home and come to university. Sometimes they move to the local area for months offering to cook and clean for their children—and keep an eye on them. We decided to act after finding some of the parents arranged to sleep in their children's dormitory with them, which of course is unacceptable. We now give them a blanket and a place to wash and eat free of charge."[25]

We've been hearing more about "helicopter parents" in the last few years. Is this just a healthy concern for the well-being of our children? Can we help them be excellent by giving them all our time, advice, and resources? Unfortunately it's pretty easy to show that students with helicopter parents tend to be "less open to new ideas and actions, as well as more vulnerable, anxious and [self-conscious], among other factors, compared with their counterparts with more distant parents." It appears this tendency leads to extended childhood and an inability to leave the nest.[26]

Do we really want to protect our children from any possible challenge? Is this the way real life works best?

Feeling uncertain, being restless, not knowing what to do, failing, making a bad career decision, or losing a job can often be a prod to a higher level of success. Eagles build a nest using thornbush strands to lock it together. Then they cover the nest with leaves and feathers to make it soft and comfortable. However, when the eaglets are about twelve weeks old, mom and dad eagles begin to remove the protection from the thorns. Pretty soon the eaglets are up on the edge of the nest to avoid the pain and discomfort. Then mom and dad eagles fly by with tasty morsels of food just out of reach. Eventually, although seeing no option other than disaster, the eaglet makes a big leap to get away from the pain and the hunger, and you know what happens. Rather than the anticipated crashing on the rocks below, he learns he can fly. I truly believe that oftentimes we encounter circumstances in our lives not to leave us in pain or hunger, but to lead us to higher levels of success than we would otherwise explore.

Years ago Joanne did a needlework that hangs in our house. It says: "There are two lasting gifts we can give to our children—one is roots, the other wings."

Roots are great, but they will start to feel like chains if not accompanied by wings. Are you giving both to your children, spouse, employees, and friends?

> Most success springs from an obstacle or failure.
> I became a cartoonist largely because I failed in
> my goal of becoming a successful executive.
> **—SCOTT ADAMS**[27]

COMFORT IS NOT EXTRAORDINARY

A couple of years ago, Ilea and I were in New York City, having dinner with some close friends. They suggested we go to a small concert down the street. I was tired from fashion industry meetings all day and had no desire to go to another concert. I was raised in Nashville. Even great concerts are a dime a dozen. On top of that, it was freezing and icy outside, and I absolutely hate the cold. There were warnings of a snowstorm as well.

However, I said I would do it because I know the potential upside of even unwelcome experiences. I made a deliberate decision to deny my momentary comfort in exchange for a possible adventure. Fortunately I've made a habit out of choosing adventure over comfort. But it's not always the easy choice.

We sat in a quaint little bar occupied by about fifty people. I really had no idea what to expect. You never really know with a concert like this. But it was snowing outside, and it really was beautiful. People were throwing snowballs in the city streets, and it looked like a moment from some whimsical New York movie scene. And on top of that, we were with good friends, having a great time talking.

We were there to see a relatively unheard of group called Fangbanger. I had never heard of them, but my friend assured me the music would be good, and I trusted his judgment on these things.

As it turned out, it was no ordinary band at all. Someone had pulled a little incognito move on us. It was none other than Sasha Dobson and Norah Jones. I have to admit; I was a bit starstruck as we were sitting maybe four feet away from Norah. Her voice was absolutely angelic. The evening was perfect and certainly created an enduring memory. Needless to say, I'm glad I stepped outside my comfort zone and made it happen.

How many adventures do you miss because of your propensity toward comfort? You stay in bed longer and miss your workout because you are more comfortable in bed for that moment. You habitually put off that big project because it's sure to be time consuming and taxing. You don't go on that trip because it sounds a little too risky. You purposely miss an event because you feel that you might be faced with too many uncomfortable questions.

You plan around your comfort, preemptively saying

no to anything that would cause you momentary discomfort. You defeat yourself before you even try. "I can't do that, I'm too scared (of discomfort)," or "I don't think I'm available that day." Why? Think of what you might be missing out on.

Think of how many times per day the people you admire deny momentary discomfort in order to achieve extraordinary levels of success. High achievers are driven by dreams, faith, and discipline.

One's level of success could be directly related to one's commitment to choosing life, adventure, and whimsy and doing the difficult thing first over settling on what is most comfortable at the time.

The habitual choice to let fear and comfort govern your decisions will surely prevent you from living an extraordinary life.

CHAPTER SEVEN

I Asked for Wonder

What do we expect from our work? If security, predictability, benefits, and retirement packages are gone, what reasons remain for a lifetime of work? What does success mean today? The full age spectrum of workers suggests that fulfillment, meaning, and wonder are more appealing and lasting than even making money. In writing about our spiritual quest, Rabbi Abraham Joshua Heschel said, "Wonder rather than doubt is the root of all knowledge."[1] Do you embrace wonder as an important element of increasing your spiritual understanding and knowledge?

I struggled with how to tell my children about Santa Claus. I was raised in a home where, with strict religious values, we would never pretend to believe something that was not true. Yet in removing anything not verifiably true, I fear we also removed some of the mystery of our faith and lives. Over the years I've softened in that position as I have seen my children and now my grandchildren enjoy the excitement of the unknown and unexplainable. I believe our opportunities for living fully are too rich to reduce them to only the things we understand completely.

Live So That You May . . .

Live so that thou mayest desire to live again—that
is thy duty—for in any case thou wilt live again!
—FRIEDRICH NIETZSCHE[2]

Good ole Friedrich was not known for his optimism about life, giving us his ideas that God is dead and man is nothing but a worm. He was plagued by depression, mental illness, and syphilis and died a lonely, disturbed man. It's hard to speculate why he wrote this quotation.

But great thoughts come from a variety of places. Using a quotable quotation does not imply a blanket endorsement of the person quoted. I like to find great ideas regardless of the source. In the Bible God used a donkey to speak wisdom,[3] and I suspect he's used a few donkeys since then as well.

Nietzsche's thought, in his own words, seems to imply a belief in life after physical death. I think that's a worthy thought and a challenge for all of us. I know I want to live my life in a way that I would want to live the same life all over again.

So I'll probably take Nietzsche's quotation, refine it a little, and make it my own. How's this: "Live your life in such a way—living, loving, and learning—that you would want to live the same life all over again."

You may do better. Take it, modify it, and make it your own. Believe me, it's an honor to be quoted. Those offended by Nietzsche or a donkey may accept it from you or me. Great ideas will reappear in many forms. In the words of CBS television news anchor, the late Walter Cronkite, "And that's the way it is."

Keep Away from These People . . .

Keep away from people who try to belittle your
ambitions. Small people always do that, but the really
great make you feel that you, too, can become great.

—MARK TWAIN[4]

No apologies are needed for selecting the people you spend
time with. Yes, we need to be compassionate and help the less
fortunate. But we also need to spend time around people who
inspire and energize us, who call us to be our best selves. One
of the key characteristics of highly successful people is that
they spend time with those who are already performing at the
level they are shooting for. While this may sound like selfishness or elitism, it's actually a matter of good stewardship of
time and resources.

In *Becoming a Person of Influence*, coauthors John Maxwell
and Jim Dornan say this: "We certainly desire for all people to
have equal access to opportunities and justice, but we know
that everyone doesn't respond equally to his environment or
advantages. And that's true for the people you will have the
opportunity to develop. Some people are eager to be enlarged.
Others don't care about personal growth or won't grow under
your care. It's your job to figure out which is which."[5]

Choosing to associate with positive, optimistic people will
accelerate our positive growth. And choosing people we truly
believe in will maximize our compassionate mentoring efforts.
We will do the most good by pouring ourselves into people
who will also grow and make a difference. We can nurture
and love hurting people. But our training and time investment

will accomplish most by working with those who are eager for a promising future, not necessarily the ones for whom we feel most sorry. Not everyone who needs what you are capable of giving will benefit from your best efforts.

REBRANDING AFRICA: SHOW SOME LOVE TO THE ENTREPRENEUR

For many years KEZA, our ethical fashion label, has focused on what the aid world refers to as *the poorest of the poor.*[6] It has become another buzz term like *sustainability* or *capacity building*. These terms help attract volunteers, donors, and public awareness.

However, in early 2010 we took a step back to analyze our methodology. We knew we were missing something that was right in front of us, partly due to inadvertently defaulting to the systems that have become the norm. But we aren't big subscribers to the norm, so we decided to shake things up a bit. We knew we could do better.

What we realized is that there are thousands of entrepreneurs all over Africa who have been working diligently to develop their businesses to the point of sustainability, and they don't get a lot of love from the aid world. They have thrashed, suffered, and pushed through the hardships, and their businesses are plugging along. But they still haven't been able to tip the scale into profitability, despite their best efforts. There are a few NGOs assisting in the arena, but they are few and far between, and typically underfunded and understaffed.

These entrepreneurs have proven their dedication

and certainly deserve our respect and attention. If their businesses grow beyond mere sustainability and really begin to thrive, they have the opportunity to make a positive impact in their communities that extends far beyond just serving their personal needs.

A thriving entrepreneurial business means a larger capacity to produce, which means more employees, more materials, and more products being exported. If these products are superior in quality and style, they can lead to positive press and a lot of public attention. All of these aspects fuel a brand of excellence and beauty, which Africa could certainly use more of.

In short, we've realized that empowering the entrepreneurial sector to grow their businesses provides them with an opportunity to employ the poorest of the poor, export more goods, and help fuel an image of excellence for their country. That image compels investors, businesspeople, and tourists to visit and invest in their country.

Anytime I'm doing development work, I'm always more excited about empowering a local to be a better leader and inspiration than I am in creating another scenario where the poor rely completely on me or the organization I represent. It seems the entrepreneurial sector is often a hub for these types of leaders.

We've realized that plenty of groups of people want food on their tables, but they aren't always willing to put in the work or create any art. So we've focused most of our efforts on those who are already paving a path. Then we come alongside them and facilitate as necessary.

I've found that we have the highest success rate, and ultimately serve a country best, by empowering the entrepreneurs and leaders rather than trying to convince a group of people who need convincing. My experience has been that these entrepreneurs and leaders have much more success convincing their own people through their example than we do with our words.

There are many ways to serve the developing world. I believe empowering the entrepreneurial sector plays a vital role in creating a solid foundation, built on indigenous businesses and wisdom, as it should be.

What if you shifted your efforts from trying to start at ground zero with the poorest of the poor to honoring the work of these entrepreneurs and supporting them so they can help raise up their communities organically?

Our role here is that of teachers and facilitators, not employers or enablers.

Just Look at Your "Friends"

When Tim Ferriss was twelve years old, an unidentified caller left this Jim Rohn quotation on his answering machine: "You are the average of the five people you spend the most time with."[7]

That message changed Tim's life forever. At only twelve years old, he recognized that the kids he was hanging out with were not the ones he wanted influencing his future. His school intensity changed. He spent his junior year in Japan studying Zen meditation. He was accepted at Princeton University where he became an all-American wrestler and a national kickboxing champion. At age twenty-three he founded BrainQUICKEN, a sports nutrition company that he then sold eight years later.[8] At age twenty-nine he wrote the best-selling book *The 4-Hour Workweek*,[9] and he is now a full-time angel investor (an affluent individual who provides capital for business start-ups).

> Pay any price to stay in the presence
> of extraordinary people.
> **—MIKE MURDOCK**[10]

So do you want to be the average of the five people you are spending the most time with? Have you gotten trapped around toxic people, people who are full-time members of the Ain't It Awful Club? People who are flag-carrying AmeriCANTS?

Years ago Brian Tracy said that one of the hallmark characteristics of successful people is spending time with those who are already performing at the level at which they want to perform. In 2002, I attended Mark Victor Hansen's MEGA Book Marketing University.[11] I spent three days with people who were already successful authors. Then I came home and did what I saw them doing. In 2005 the first edition of *48 Days to the Work You Love* was published. In 2008 I got a fat contract with the biggest publishing house in the world—Random House—to publish *No More Dreaded Mondays*. I've continued to attend writers' seminars every year and now have a blast welcoming up-and-coming writers to our popular Write to the Bank events here on our property.[12] Today I can talk to multiple publishers about any book idea I may have. I'm not smarter, faster, or better looking; I just spent time around people who were already living the life I wanted to live.

Change Your Stars?

Walking through the casinos in Reno recently reminded me of the many poorly thought-out ways that people try to improve their positions in life. I'd like to think that the people there are just having a little harmless fun, maybe spending twenty dollars in the same way you would ride the roller coaster just for the thrill of it. And yet I don't see that simple enjoyment in these people sitting in front of the slot machines hour after hour. The desperation in their tired faces clearly shows they really do believe that luck may smile on them and give them an unexpected and undeserved payout.

What if they spent the same time and money in a direction that had more planning and a realistic chance for success? What if they had taken the five hundred dollars they blew last night and purchased a lawn mower and started a landscape business? Or if they had spent that on a six-week course to learn the eBay business model? Or to purchase the tools to fulfill a lifelong dream of being a wood carver? They could print up some flyers to announce a delivery service for the elderly as my dad did until he was eighty-eight years old. The list of real opportunities for changing your stars is endless.[13]

No matter how limited our resources, we all make daily choices. Are you spending your resources on consumptive living, gambling them away on risky ventures, or investing them in carefully laid-out plans for the future you want? The decisions you're making today are setting the stage for where you'll be five years from now. If a slot machine or roulette wheel plays any part in determining your future, you have likely thrown your chances for a meaningful, fulfilling, and profitable life into the wind.

Embracing mystery and wonder in life does not mean living in an unrealistic fantasy world, waiting for fate or luck to determine your future. On the contrary, it means carefully planning to release your strongest gifts, your most unique talents, in ways that will bring hope and encouragement to the world in a manner only you can fulfill.

WE CAN ALL LIVE IN WONDERLAND

I've heard statements like, "Jared lives in his own little world," since I was a toddler. As I've grown older, I've learned that people really mean, "Jared doesn't live in reality." I disagree.

I believe the world is exactly what we make it. We create our own reality with every choice we make. What may be steadfast and true in my reality may be entirely absurd in someone else's.

Bob Goff invents holidays, unites world leaders, incites parades, brings justice to Uganda, gets people out of their comfort zones, creates peace treaties, and defines a lasting good-bye when he and his family jump fully clothed into the lake, waving as others sail away in a boat.[14] Bob knows how to create a beautiful reality around him that inevitably touches the lives and hearts of others. Bob is making it happen. He's living deliberately in his own little Wonderland. Godspeed, Bob!

I recognize that this is more representative of lunacy than reality for most people. However, I believe it's a choice. People like Bob scare the status quo. Others will find comfort in writing him off as a loon. But I believe Bob is one of the few who actually has things figured out. He's living the way God created him to live, whimsically floating through life as he fosters more love, equality, peace, community, and happiness across the globe.

Isaac Newton claimed that things have an alternate reality separate from our perception of them. Quantum physics reveals that as our perception of an object changes, the object itself actually changes according to that perception.

Ultimately all creation is expressed through the mind and how we perceive reality.

I believe our greatest tool for changing the world is changing the way we perceive it. I choose to create a reality where an egalitarian society is probable, rather than choose to believe the more pervasive notion that the world is hopelessly doomed to self-destruct. This perception plays a key role in my Wonderland.

I live in a world full of dreams, faith, and whimsy, where anything is possible. Relationships always trump trivial things like time, money, and comfort. Each step of life is raw and deliberate. I believe loyalty, vulnerability, and honesty to be among the most imperative characteristics. And I believe there is purpose to everything.

Every day I am creating my little Wonderland and constantly sailing away from the safety of the shore, as Twain would put it. I believe that's where we find our most beautiful experiences and relationships. People are so prone to limiting themselves because they believe they have to conform to the rules that society has created around them. Not true. Those rules typically leave no room for innovation, surprise, or joy. If you want to live in Wonderland, you have to be willing to create it, foster it, and dwell within it.

I'm convinced that most people considered to be crazy are actually the ones who really get it. (Tom Waits, you are Leviticusly Deuteronomous.[15])

I think the secret to happiness is wrapped up in a person's willingness to live a life of whimsy and Ubuntu.[16] Mariachi music also helps.

Alice in Suburbia might have been a bit of a letdown. It's Wonderland that intrigues us—the mystery, the adventure, and the Mad Hatter—leaving us wide-eyed and awestruck. The first step to getting there is to recognize and embrace the fact that we all have the ability to live there. But we have to be willing to let go of the desire to fit in to the status quo. You can be normal, or you can live in Wonderland. Your choice. But you can't have both.

I choose Wonderland.

Better Death than This . . .

As a child Leonardo da Vinci had an intense curiosity about birds and flight. He studied their wings and modeled helicopters, parachutes, and flying machines based on their anatomy. The freedom and movement of birds served as a metaphor for his life. He observed poetically that a mother goldfinch, seeing her babies in a cage, would feed them a bit of a poisonous plant, noting,  "Better death than to be without freedom."[17]

In the course of his frequent strolls through the streets of Florence, da Vinci often encountered merchants selling caged birds. Frequently he stopped, paid the purchase price, then opened the door of the cage and released the birds to the endless blue sky. For da Vinci, his constant search for knowledge served as the open door to his freedom.

Are you living in a cage? If you are, is it one that has been imposed on you, or is it of your own making?

Are you stuck in a job that keeps a lid on your talents?

Did you read several good books last year? Visit another community, state, or country?

Have you taken a class on a new subject or made friends with someone of another faith?

Have you allowed fear and anger to create a prison of your own making?

Just try the door; it may not actually be locked. You can add your comments at 48Days.com[18] regarding your personal experience of being caged.

Stay Hungry. Stay Foolish.

The Whole Earth Catalog was a catalog of earth-friendly, innovative, and fun products for the hippie generation. On the back cover of the final 1974 edition of *The Whole Earth Catalog* was the famous saying: "Stay Hungry. Stay Foolish." But now that saying has remained popular because of the closing comments in Steve Jobs's 2005 commencement speech at Stanford University: "Stay Hungry. Stay Foolish. And I have always wished that for myself. And now, as you graduate to begin anew, I wish that for you."[19]

Expecting wonder in your life will look foolish to some. Those who desire that life be a logical, analytical, sequential process of birth to death will likely criticize you for wanting wonder—the unexplainable but profoundly exhilarating things in life.

He who can no longer pause to wonder and stand rapt in awe, is as good as dead, his eyes are closed.
—ALBERT EINSTEIN[20]

Go Ahead; Astonish Me

Astonish is not a word we hear much. But what do you do that is brilliant, amazing, excellent, remarkable, essential, extraordinary, outstanding, noteworthy, incredible, or astonishing?

What displays your personal best—your personal brilliance?

The story is told that one day the great artist Picasso was walking in the market. A woman approached him, handed him a pencil and piece of paper, and asked, "Can you do a little drawing for me?"

Picasso replied, "Absolutely." He did a quick little drawing and handed it back to the woman.

She looked at it and said, "That's amazing." After thanking him she started to walk away.

Picasso stopped her and said, "Excuse me, that'll be one million dollars."

She said, "One million dollars? That took you thirty seconds."

Picasso replied, "My dear lady, it took me thirty years to do that."

There are only three legs to extraordinary success:

1. What are you deeply passionate about?
2. How can you do that with excellence, perhaps better than anyone else?
3. What's your economic model? How are you generating income?

Integrating these three components will separate you from 97 percent of the people on the face of the earth. How can you be the Bill Gates, Mick Jagger, Bono, Mother Teresa, or Billy Graham in your area of passion? Don't let false humility keep you from sharing your best with the world. Go ahead; astonish me.

Hope Deferred Makes the Heart Sick

At the beginning of each year we hear lots of people talk about their hopes and dreams for next year. And yet some of those same people see the next year come and go with no noticeable change in their lives. Why do some people dream, but their lives never change, while others dream and walk into new successes every day? A comment on a 48 Days blog shared about how "liberating" it was to live a creative, entrepreneurial life. And then the commenter added, "Admittedly, I speak not from experience, but anticipation."[21]

How do we move from anticipation to real experience?

Let's walk through the process:

1. Imagination
2. Dreaming
3. Anticipation
4. Goal setting (creating a timeline)
5. Plan of action
6. Action
7. Changed life—dreams realized

It should be easy to find where you are in this sequence.

Anticipation can be exhilarating. But it will turn to bitterness and anger if you get stuck there.

Remember Proverbs 13:12: "Hope deferred makes the heart sick, but a longing fulfilled is a tree of life" (NIV).

SWEET DISCIPLINE

I believe that most anything worth having or achieving typically comes as a result of discipline and often only after some heartache and pain. Want to be a doctor? You had better be prepared to spend the first half of your life in school and the second half paying off the expense while tending to the sick. That's not an easy process, but it can certainly be fulfilling.

I work out daily because I want my body to perform optimally. Optimal physical performance allows me to achieve the things I believe are most important and live the life I want. When I was learning Kinyarwanda, I disciplined myself to learn and speak it even when it was much easier to just use a translator. It was part of my commitment to understanding the Rwandan culture, being able to communicate effectively and ultimately learning how to serve Rwanda best.

I've poured my heart and soul into many entrepreneurial businesses over the years, making many sacrifices along the way. Sacrifice, in and of itself, implies an act of discipline. In many ways, discipline is synonymous with perseverance.

Conditioning myself to employing a worldview perspective is a discipline that affords me a great deal of peace and balance. I've disciplined myself to always see the positive in life. That perspective has become my system default. My first reaction to a problem is a positive one rather than the typical negative one.

It took a lot of practice and discipline to embrace my father's wisdom in the question, "Do you have a problem or an opportunity for a solution?" Years later, I see problems in that light, and they don't debilitate me. Rarely do they even cause me to hesitate. I automatically see the opportunity to learn something, create a better solution than I had thought of before, or take an entirely new path.

It takes a lot of discipline to foster a healthy relationship. If I don't prevent myself from reacting in anger or frustration, it causes serious problems. I have to choose to remain calm, be understanding, and always value relationships above all else in life. This discipline has provided me with an absolutely beautiful marriage and many thriving relationships that I cherish.

Can you think of anything negative that comes from self-discipline? Sure, there are extremes to everything, but generally speaking, self-discipline results in more happiness and fulfillment.

Discipline leads to achievement. Consistent achievement leads to self-confidence, which leads to a higher quality of life and a sense of purpose. In the absence of discipline, I feel life is living me rather than me deliberately seizing each moment of the day and getting the most out of life.

Martin Luther King Jr., Nelson Mandela, Mother Teresa, and Mahatma Gandhi were disciplined. They certainly would not have lived the extraordinary lives they lived without it. Their fulfillment largely relied on it. Even the mere knowledge that I am habitually a disciplined person empowers me to do more and be more.

Discipline is an ongoing, deliberate commitment. It's a direct reflection of my ethos and intention.

I believe the sweetest things in life are a result of discipline. And when I operate from that perspective, disciplining myself to achieve my goals gets easier and easier.

Can I become a great boxer without discipline? Can I have a healthy marriage without it? Could I write this book without it? When I reflect on all my greatest experiences and accomplishments in life, I can easily see that they came as a result of consistent discipline.

It provides a path to achieving the things I want in life. Thriving relationships, a strong, resilient body, self-confidence, inner peace, life balance, understanding, and wisdom are results of discipline.

The more discipline I employ in my life, the sweeter life becomes.

How does discipline play a role in your life? Can you connect your level of discipline to your quality of life?

Want to Be Intelligent and Average or Creative and Successful?

Studies over the last fifty years show children increasing in IQ. But since 1990, scores of creativity have gone down. Children *and* adults are becoming less creative.[22]

The accepted definition of *creativity* is production of something original and useful. Too much TV, video games, and time indoors can be blamed, but standardized tests and the push to accumulate facts have added to the decline.

In adulthood, creativity will open more opportunities than intelligence will. Those with high GPAs may have more traditional doors open to them, while those with a lower GPA may initiate the search for a more authentic and successful career path.

Here are some things we can do as adults to kill creativity and idea generation:

1. Wallow in self-pity.
2. Blame others.
3. Give up on dreams.
4. Overreact to criticism.
5. Underestimate our opportunities.

Here are some ways we can increase creativity:

1. Laugh out loud every day.
2. Break familiar routines.
3. Say to ourselves, "I can do this."
4. Set aside fifteen minutes daily for thinking.
5. Read one nonfiction book a month.

Unusually Unusual

This is actually the title of a popular country song by Lonestar from the album *I'm Already There*. The refrain to the song begins, "She's unusually unusual, absolutely unpredictable,"[23] and every time I hear it I think of about twenty of my favorite people. Jared certainly fits in this category. His clothes, music, and habits have never been usual. But what he adds to our family interactions is priceless. My grandson, Caleb, who at sixteen is exploring his true interests, will not likely be usual. While his basketball team members are driving down the court, Caleb may notice a pretty bird sitting in the window. One of my favorite counselors has been known to ask a client to take silent communion with her rather than talk. My friend the theologian challenges lots of usual Christian thinking. A woman carved two magnificent faces on a dead tree in our yard. It's not likely her high school guidance counselor suggested "tree carver" as a career path. The research that Thomas Stanley did for his book *The Millionaire*

Mind reveals that people whose grades will not allow them to attend graduate school often end up in unusual work and careers that are a more authentic fit and lead to millionaire status.[24]

You likely have some characteristics that make you unusually unusual. Your interests in food, art, music, hobbies, and work confirm that you will never be normal. But then again, greatness is never normal. Enjoy the journey!

Dreamers of the Day

Your dreams may be the real beginnings of the future you want.

In *Seven Pillars of Wisdom*, T. E. Lawrence says, "All men dream: but not equally. Those who dream by night in the dusty recesses of their minds wake in the day to find that it was vanity: but the dreamers of the day are dangerous men, for they may act their dream with open eyes, to make it possible."[25]

Now there's a clear picture. "Dreamers of the day" are dangerous because they "act their dream with open eyes, to make it possible." We heard a lot about dreams during the 2008 elections. As our new president, Barack Obama inspired people to think big and never stop believing that big dreams can come true. Certainly his life story is a clear example of that.

In today's sophisticated, technological world we often dismiss our night dreams as the result of consuming too much pizza or having too much on our minds when we went to bed. But what about those daydreams? Are they to be dismissed as random thoughts passing through our brains? Should we pay attention to those dreams or just hunker down and be realistic and practical with the economy in the shape it is? With jobs being lost, homes being foreclosed, $700 billion up in smoke, and major corporations on the brink of disaster, surely now is not the time to dream. Or is it? Haven't you experienced in your life how those times of trials often release your best ideas? Have you ever taken a dream and acted it into reality? Where have your best ideas started?

Could your dreams of the day be the seeds of creative solutions and the opening door into your greatest new opportunities?

> Cherish your visions and your dreams as they are the children of your soul, the blueprints of your ultimate achievements.
> —NAPOLEON HILL[26]

Nothing concerns me as a life coach more than beginning the coaching process with someone who says he has no dreams. Having no dreams traps people in jobs they hate, relationships that have never blossomed, and cars, houses, and clothes that serve nothing but utilitarian functions.

Don't underestimate the value of your night dreams as well, for problem solving and creative approaches to your situation. And by all means, keep dreaming during the day. Tap into those recurring thoughts and ideas that have followed you for years.

> All successful men and women are big dreamers. They imagine what their future could be, ideal in every respect, and then they work every day toward their distant vision, that goal or purpose.
> —BRIAN TRACY[27]

If you can't dream it, it won't likely happen. Success doesn't sneak up on us. It starts as a dream that we combine with a clear plan of action. Become a dreamer of the day, and watch your success soar. Take to heart the words of Carl Sandburg: "Nothing happens unless first a dream."[28]

What is a recurring dream that you have had?

Could it be the seed for a direction God wants you to move in?

> Hold fast to dreams,
> For if dreams die,
> Life is a broken-winged bird
> That cannot fly.
> **—LANGSTON HUGHES**[29]

How Old Are You?

On the 48Days.net website a member asked, "I'm thirty-seven. Is it too late for me?" I have seen people who at thirty-seven seemed old, and I have seen those who at ninety-one have a twinkle in their eyes and the excitement of future plans. This quotation by General Douglas MacArthur is a poignant overview of the source of aging:

Youth is not a period of time. It is a state of mind, a result of the will, a quality of the imagination, a victory of courage over timidity, of the taste for adventure over the love of comfort. A man doesn't grow old because he has lived a certain number of years. A man grows old when he deserts his ideal. *The years may wrinkle his skin, but deserting his ideal wrinkles his soul. Preoccupations, fears, doubts, and despair are the enemies which slowly bow us toward earth and turn us into dust before death.* You will remain young as long as you are open to what is beautiful, good and great; receptive to the messages of other men and women, of nature and of God. *If one day you should become bitter, pessimistic, and gnawed by despair, may God have mercy on your old man's soul.*[30]

Keep yourself young by having goals that inspire you, friends who ignite your imagination, and work that engages your passions.

Have a Curious Child?

William and Mary had three children, two daughters named Kristi and Libby and a son they nicknamed Trey. Since William was a successful Seattle attorney and Mary was a schoolteacher, they thought a career in law would be an appropriate pursuit for their only son as well.

Imagine their pleasure when Trey scored 1590 out of a possible 1600 on the SAT. His parents were thrilled when he was accepted into Harvard in 1973. But Trey had a hard time finding a clear focus for his studies and spent most of his time playing around on the school's computers.

According to Trey's parents, they were "sick when Trey told us he planned to leave college to take advantage of a window of opportunity he believed would be long gone by the time he graduated from Harvard."[31] Much to the dismay of his parents, he dropped out of school forever in 1975.

In his book, *Showing Up for Life*, Trey's dad explains the lesson he learned as a father: "Perhaps there's a lesson in this for parents of other curious children who, from the start, require the freedom to meet life on their own terms: It is that there is no statute of limitations on the dreams you have for your children.

And there is no way to predict how much delight you might feel when those dreams are realized in a far different way than you could have imagined."[32]

Incidentally, Trey was chosen as a nickname because this son was the third William in the family tree. You may know him by his adult name, Bill Gates.[33]

Sew Up Your Buttonholes?

Maybe you need to brush your teeth with your left hand today!

This comes from a story I read in the little classic book *I Dare You!* by William H. Danforth:

> Once a professor hit upon a great discovery while buttoning up his vest. Or rather, he hit upon the discovery because his vest wouldn't button up. His little daughter had sewn up some of the button-holes. His fingers were going along as usual in their most intricate operations of buttoning a button . . . when something happened. A button wouldn't button.
>
> The fingers fumbled helplessly for a moment, then sent out a call for help. *The mind woke up.* The eyes looked down . . . a new idea was born, or rather a new understanding of an old idea. What the professor had discovered was that fingers can remember.[34]

You know how automatic things can become, such as riding a bicycle, using a keyboard, or even driving home from the office. The story continued, "Then [the professor] began playing pranks on his classes, and he found that the answer was always the same. *As long as they could keep on doing the things they had always done, their minds wouldn't work. It was only* when he figuratively sewed up their button-holes, stole their notebooks, locked the doors, upset their routine . . . that any thinking was done."[35]

The professor came to the "great, and now generally accepted, conclusion that the mind of man is 'an emergency organ.'" It "relegates everything possible" to automatic functions of the body "as long as it is able," and "it is only when the old order of things won't work any longer that it gets on the job" and starts working. Keeping things the same may be keeping you stupid.[37]

A lot of what we think of as neurosis in this country
is simply people who are unhappy because
they're not using their creative resources.
—JULIA CAMERON[36]

Research shows that 90 percent of five-year-olds
are creative, but only 2 percent of adults are.
—LEE LILBER[38]

So my advice is this: sew up some buttonholes in your life. Drive a different route home from work. Read a book you would not normally read. Write your name with the hand opposite your normal dominance to see how it wakes up your brain. Take time to stop and help a stranded motorist. Volunteer to help on a community project. And welcome the unexpected closed buttonholes this week. You may be surprised at having your brain turn on. Who knows what creative ideas or solutions you may discover. You may even brighten up your face!

Who is like the wise man?
Who knows the explanation of things?
Wisdom brightens a man's face
and changes its hard appearance.
—ECCLESIASTES 8:1 (NIV)

What could you do today to wake up your mind?

Try Following What Amuses Your Mind

Jared failed pretty miserably in the public school classroom. We removed him from that "harsh" environment, where they demanded that he know physics and mathematics from a book to be well-rounded and educated. When he was fourteen, I bought a 1968 VW Karmann Ghia for Jared's first car. Together we sanded the body and ultimately painted it ourselves—Porsche

Guards Red. We replaced the interior carpeting, all the rubber around the glass, and most of the exterior chrome. We pulled the engine and supertuned it from top to bottom. Jared learned about electrical systems, internal combustion, brake systems, and oh, yes, physics and mathematics in the process. The resulting eye-popping ride was a source of pride and knowledge for Jared because it was also a focus for his pleasure. And it gave him the framework for helping others find unique expressions of their God-given talents.[39]

Bill Gates, Michael Dell, Oprah Winfrey, Michelangelo, Henry David Thoreau, Angelina Jolie, Donald Trump, Justin Bieber, and Mr. Rogers all seemed to have developed what amused their minds.

Are you trying to grow by submitting yourself to force and harshness, or are you paying attention to what amuses your mind? Have you bought into the common philosophy that if you enjoy something, you certainly can't make a living with that as a focus? Why don't you stop beating yourself up and follow your passions? You just might go directly toward success.

> Do not, then, train [youth] to learning by force and harshness; but direct them to it by what amuses their minds, so that you may be the better able to discover with accuracy the peculiar bent of the genius of each.
> —PLATO[40]

People Think I'm Crazy

In the movie *The Pursuit of Happyness*, there is a real-life line from the movie's character inspiration, Chris Gardner. His mother used to tell him, "Don't ever let someone else tell you what you can't do. Not even me." Chris explains, "When someone says, 'You can't,' what it really means is *they* can't—so why should *you* get to?"[41]

Everyone knows about starving artists and writers. And yeah, you know what to do when a musician knocks on your door: pay him and take the pizza.

Okay, so you know your calling and have your dream to bring it to life. But people say you're crazy. Do you have a clear plan for making the work you'll be doing profitable? Have you created a transition from what you're doing now so you don't end up living on the street? As long as you have a plan for how you'll move forward, don't allow jealous onlookers to push their insecurities and indecision into the life you want to live.

In my weekly podcast I often use the first few bars from John Lennon's song *Watching the Wheels* that is on the album *Double Fantasy*: "People say I'm crazy doing what I'm doing." I think that conveys pretty clearly the sentiments of people looking on when you are doing something creative, astonishing, amazing, wonderful, and potentially world changing.

SNOW GLOBES

In America, the land of freedom, there is a tendency to create a Snow Globe world. People create a way of life that is comfortable and safe. They find others with similar beliefs and lifestyles and develop a culture, a religion, or even a neighborhood. We often refer to their dwellings as "the suburbs." Anything outside the Snow Globe is generally believed to be scary, off-limits, unattainable, and downright crazy.

Snow Globers spend most of their lives creating

parameters and limitations for themselves. They say, "I cannot do this because. . . . We cannot go there because it's dangerous." There's a lot of fear involved, but it's typically overshadowed by the perceived appearance of success via material wealth or achievement. They are not ignorant of this dynamic either; it is a deliberate practice.

Comfort, security (jobs, finances, relationships), and normalcy are the cornerstones of the Snow Globe. Snow Globers share a sacred agreement that taking risks, thinking outside the box, traveling the world, and not having a nine-to-five job and a 401(k) are reckless and irresponsible. "Impossible" is the excuse most commonly used to describe dreams and ideas outside the Snow Globe. This mentality often develops and fosters an underlying myopic "us and them" doctrine, separating them from humanity.

Snow Globers would have radically disapproved of revolutionaries such as Einstein, Galileo, Gandhi, Pollock, and Gates during their journeys. These guys took huge risks and lived far beyond the bounds of the Snow Globe. They believed in crazy ideas developed in their garages. They viewed risk as a key component to their success rather than something to be avoided like the plague. They were ostracized and condemned for habitual defiance of the status quo. They were outcasts because of their resistance to live in the Snow Globe.

These types of people represent the crazies who believe we are all interconnected and anything is possible when we believe and stand together. They don't let fear or limitations detour them from anything they believe in. Society calls them irresponsible, delusional, and reckless. But I believe they were living the way we were created to live: boundless and free.

Every man dies; not every man really lives.
—WILLIAM WALLACE IN *BRAVEHEART*[42]

If Your Life Is Not Working, Try This

I have lots of opportunities to write for magazines. An editor of *Success* asked me: "Dan, I'm looking for a checklist of sorts . . . once you've figured out that life isn't working, what are the steps to reshaping your work or creating a new opportunity?"

I responded immediately. Here's what I recommended:

1. Look inward first. Eighty-five percent of the process of having the confidence of an authentic fit in your career comes from looking inward first. We get the cart before the horse by looking at who's hiring or searching out the hottest business opportunities.
2. Trust your passions. Don't be deterred because you've been told your idea is not realistic or practical. Passion drives success in unusual ventures.
3. Create a clear plan of action. Passion and enthusiasm alone are not enough. You need a strategy and a timeline.
4. Look forward. Discouragement, resentment, guilt, and depression are emotions connected with looking at the past—what you are coming *from*. Confidence, enthusiasm, and boldness overtake those negative emotions as you become clear about what you are moving *to*.

5. Commit to one year of focused action without looking back.

You can make corrections no matter where you find yourself on the road of life. It's never too late to create a new beginning. Making good decisions can overcome many effects of bad ones.

Don't Be This Optimistic—Things Are Going to Get Worse

I read a blog from a guy who said he suffers from "pathological optimism"—a belief that everything can be turned around if you want to turn things around. But he also suffers from stress, tension, and depression. And now he's wondering if his pathological optimism has produced an equal but destructive shadow side.

Is that the way it works? Do we expect opposites in all areas of our lives?

As the film *Shadowlands* concludes, C. S. Lewis laments, "Why love if losing hurts so much? I have no answers. . . . The pain now is part of the happiness then. That's the deal."[43]

Is it a risk to be too optimistic? Will a sense of wonder set us up for major reality disappointments? Here's a short comment from a professor at Jefferson Medical College on the issue. See if this psychological garbage cheers you up:

> Fantasies whose core is constituted by the notions of "someday" and "if only" are ubiquitous in human psyche. In severe character pathology, however, these fantasies have a particularly tenacious, defensive, and ego-depleting quality. The "someday" fantasy idealizes the future and fosters optimism, and the "if only" fantasy idealizes the past and lays

the groundwork for nostalgia. The two fantasies originate in the narcissistic disequilibrium consequent upon the early mother-child separation experiences, though the oedipal conflict also contributes to them.[44]

The professor suggests some cures for optimism, including "rupturing the patient's excessive hope, and reconstructing the early scenarios underlying the need for excessive hope."

Well, isn't that special? Is it pathological to expect goodness from the person you meet in a dark alley, to believe a child can rise from the ghetto and do something great, to see hope in the midst of earthquakes, tsunamis, and wars? Is it false optimism to follow your dream?

Apparently some childhood trauma—probably the severe way in which I was potty-trained—caused me to have "excessive hope." Whatever. Call off the shrinks; forget the psychotropic drugs. Just leave me alone with my fantasies and wonder. Don't take away my "someday" and "if only." If you don't "rupture my excessive hope," I won't poke a hole in yours. I'll take the risk of competing emotions. Just let me enjoy my pathological optimism.

What about you?

Do you suffer from optimism?

Do you ask for wonder?

> The real voyage of discovery consists not in
> seeking new landscapes but in having new eyes.
> **—MARCEL PROUST**[45]

CHAPTER EIGHT

Not (Only) for Profit

W e've seen Jeff Skoll (eBay), Mark Zuckerberg (Facebook), Bill Gates (Microsoft), Warren Buffett (Berkshire Hathaway), Michael Bloomberg (New York City mayor and founder of Bloomberg financial news service), and others commit to the Giving Pledge—pledging to give away at least half of their wealth to philanthropic causes.[1] Yes, these individuals built for-profit businesses but then structured those profits to be plowed into worthy endeavors. Their positive leadership in this area has caused a healthy blurring of the distinctions between for-profit and nonprofit businesses. New entities under titles like social entrepreneurship and ethical capitalism are emerging from those who are twenty-six or seventy-six years old.

Not-Only-for-Profit

Not all businesspeople are greedy. We've heard the Bernie Madoff phony investment stories, heard about banks that lend to unqualified candidates, and seen the get-rich-quick promises on late-night TV. It's easy to quickly classify all businesspeople or for-profit companies as greedy. While making money can be an altruistic endeavor to equip and provide for others, greed is typically a shortsighted model for taking advantage of others.

But on the other side of greed is the fear of money. Too many people shun the idea of making money as evil and believe good can be done only by nonprofits. Unfortunately many individuals who self-righteously bury themselves in nonprofit organizations spend 80 percent of their precious time begging for money in lieu of working on the cause about which they are passionate. Don't get caught in the delusion that being destitute is a necessary framework for helping the world. In fact, it will hamper your ability to do so. Money is like fire: it can burn you and leave you disfigured, or it can keep you warm and safe.

Since Adam Smith, the author of *The Wealth of Nations* (1776), economists have understood that self-love leads to quality products and social benefits. If a baker makes wonderful bread, he brings nutrition and pleasure to the community as well as financial rewards for himself and his family. It is not his benevolence but self-interest that provides the most benefits for everyone involved. And there can be true, authentic benevolence as well.

Good intentions and a pure and giving heart are not enough. Economic accountability is a good thing. If an organization's efforts are secured by God, the government, or the heartstrings of generous individuals, it can be run inefficiently with little measurement of accomplishment. The businessman has no such cushion. Either something of value and fair exchange is produced and delivered, or the business will not survive. In that sense, the business model requires more honesty and transparency than the nonprofit model.

I love running a business. I love not being handcuffed by a publicly traded board of directors or by the required board for a nonprofit organization. We can make decisions quickly about giving and blessing—and about sound financial opportunities.

I am deeply grateful and feel privileged to be able to have a not-only-for-profit company.

How would you categorize your work or business?

I Can't Make Money. Will You Give Me Some?

It seems that every day I hear from someone who is starting another nonprofit business or ministry and wants me to contribute money. And along with that, there is usually the implication that the nonprofit has a higher calling and more godliness than any business that makes money could possibly have. Do you really think that just because an organization lists itself as nonprofit, it is doing work that is more worthwhile than a regular for-profit one?

No, I observe that many people ignore the basics of making any organization great and simply hope that others will fund their lack of business skills and inefficiency. In a follow-up to *Good to Great*,[2] author Jim Collins said any organization must blend three components: (1) What is your passion? (2) What can you do with excellence? and (3) What is your economic model? Lacking clarity in any of those will cause you to fail.

Think about it as in this model:

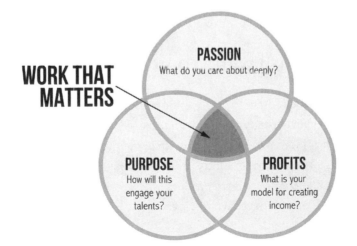

WORK THAT MATTERS

PASSION
What do you care about deeply?

PURPOSE
How will this engage your talents?

PROFITS
What is your model for creating income?

You must have all three legs to this stool. Missing any one will not describe work that releases your very best.

For-profits go out of business all the time and rightfully so. Poor financial controls, inability to adapt, fierce competition, ineffective management, and desire to move on contribute to the rapid closing of businesses. Often a purpose was completed or a window of opportunity has passed, and the business closes its doors peacefully.

No organization should exist simply to exist. In a *Fast Company* article, "Why Charities Should Have an Expiration Date," Nancy Lublin said, "A non-profit exists to cure something, address an issue, or elevate the status of a group of people; if and when that's achieved, we should be done."[3] If the purpose has been accomplished, new methods have made it obsolete, no self-sustaining economic model is in place, or management is ineffective, any organization should cease to exist. Don't expect to use guilt or pity as your method of funding your operation. Ethical capitalism is an honorable form of doing good in the world.

And no, being unemployed for a long period of time is probably not God's way of telling you to start a nonprofit. Prove you can make money in the real world and you can fund any good works you are drawn to.

IF I WANT TO DO MORE

Clients who come to me wanting to do more than just support an already existing charity often ask me about starting their own charity or social venture that would serve a developing country. I typically have one standard reply: if you want to serve a developing country (or group of people), you have two choices.

First, drop everything you're doing, move there, live among them, learn what they need, listen, learn, dive deep into their culture, eat their food, learn their language, and become one with them. Commit to at least five years for this process. Do it because you can't fathom *not* doing it. Don't do it because you're in love with the cause. Do it because you're in love with the people in need. They are your family, just as real and true as your own blood. Do it because this is who you are, who you were created to be.

Second, support someone else who is already doing everything I just mentioned. It takes a considerable amount of effort to just find someone like this, ensure his or her integrity and character, establish a relationship, create systems for accountability, and develop a support structure. Then you have to maintain that relationship on an ongoing basis. Many people cannot follow through even on this commitment. It takes time, patience, money, and a lot of understanding on your side. It's also going to require you to trust, and that's no small feat.

Don't start another organization, nonprofit or for-profit, just because you see a need. Thousands of altruists out there have already put in years and years of work, and they understand what needs to be done much better than you could ever fathom. Honor their work by supporting them.

By deviating from these two options, you are at great risk of either dishonoring someone else's lifelong mission or contributing more to the problem rather than the solution. It's mind-boggling how many people believe that they can solve issues like world hunger or HIV by halfheartedly being involved. Maybe they saw a tearjerker film or got one too many e-mails from Compassion International, and now they want to start a new nonprofit.

There are currently 1.9 million nonprofits in the United States alone. The IRS approves tax exemption for new groups every ten to fifteen minutes, resulting in about fifty thousand new nonprofits per year.[4] Half of these groups are redundant, inefficiently and often ineffectively chasing down the same goals as their neighbors.[5]

There is a reason it takes almost twenty-four years of formal education to become a doctor. If you're going to be operating on someone, it's best that you make a lifestyle of it. The same should be true of aiding a developing country or people group. If you want to become a doctor after high school, you go back to school for another twelve years.

But if you want to become a humanitarian in Africa, just hop on a plane and hope for the best. What?

If you really want to help, either go all in or be willing to put in the effort to find someone else who has and support his or her work. Either way, if you really want to be effective, you have to put in some serious time.

Educate yourself endlessly. Listen relentlessly. And then teach. The most effective philanthropy is the type that teaches its beneficiaries to think for themselves and ultimately solve their own problems. If you're not working yourself out of a job, you're failing.

Is It Okay to Make Money from a Christian Website?

A member of 48Days.net asked this question: "Is it really ok to make money from a ministry or Christian based website? . . . For some reason I feel I need confirmation that it's ok to profit from the things of God."[6]

And here's my response: You raise a question that has been

an elephant in the room for Christians all through history. I think the issue is not whether or not you can make money from a Christian website as much as it is: "Am I serving people or taking advantage of them?" If you are truly serving people, then the transfer of money is a wonderful spiritual exchange. Money is created, and everyone involved is better off as a result.

If someone buys a copy of *48 Days to the Work You Love*, I now have $20 to feed my family. If that person is simply $20 poorer, there is nothing Christian about that exchange. But my hope is that the information will add $50,000 to the person's income next year and allow him or her to bless others with that increase.

When Jesus drove the merchants out of the temple, he knew they were taking advantage of people. They were out to rob and cheat the people who were coming to worship and didn't know the rates of exchange in that community. They were charging unreasonable prices to purchase animals and exchange the foreign currency of those who came with pure hearts to worship God at the temple and fulfill the laws as given through Moses.

So the question posed concerns the attitude of the heart—whether we're selling Mercedes cars or Bibles.

I don't think we have to call a business *Christian* if we're providing products and services at reasonable prices. Our Christian witness will find a receptive heart if we've treated someone with respect and fairness. Unfortunately it seems many people call their businesses *Christian* in the hope that customers will overlook poor quality and unreliable service.

If I have a landscape business or sell from an organic garden or teach at the local university, I am positioning myself to "profit from the things of God." We are all part of the same marvelous world; providing religious information is not more Christian than selling fresh brown eggs. I trust that we are all concerned about how we are making money and are asking ourselves daily if Jesus would do what we're doing. Remember, he was a carpenter, and someone had to pay for his services. What do you think a chair made by Jesus would look like?

I had the privilege of meeting Tom Szaky, founder of TerraCycle.[7] What an exciting business! It recycles the nastiest trash available and turns it into organic fertilizer that is sold at Target, Home Depot, and other retailers. The business model is totally for-profit, yet the company is changing the world in the way we view trash and raising millions for charities. I think we're seeing a positive correction from the American corporations that have been raping their communities and customers. The Internet has made everyone more transparent with fewer opportunities to hide behind shady business practices.

Bottom line: I think the legal structure we choose is less important than having a worthy mission to fulfill. Your mission will drive how you do business, regardless of what it's called.

THE INDUSTRY OF AID: INSPIRE ME

I just read an excerpt from a book titled *The Last Lecture*. Randy Pausch said, "When you use money to fight poverty, it can be of great value, but too often, you're working at the margins. When you're putting people on the moon, you're inspiring all of us to achieve the maximum of human potential, which is how our greatest problems will eventually be solved."[8]

I think something is worth noting there. We need both, but people need to be inspired to do more, be more, and experience more. Not to collect more things, and not to be discontent, but to get more life out of life. To truly live.

And let's face it; a great inspirational story like *Rocky*, *Braveheart*, or *The Pursuit of Happyness* can do that. We find ourselves seriously compelled to work out, free the people, or pursue our dream career because we see that there is more out there and that it's possible to achieve. We are reminded once again that even ordinary people are capable of extraordinary things. We need that.

Why have organizations like **charity: water** and Invisible Children done so well?[9] Because they have inspired us. They have taken what were previously insurmountable epidemics and provided us with clear, tangible methods for addressing them. And then they show us the fruits of our efforts. That's a game changer.

Scott Harrison of **charity: water** realized that just mastering and sharing the facts about the lack of clean water for the poor are not enough. He needed a better story. So he found a way to inspire us. When you watch his inspiring videos, you don't feel sad; you feel inspired.[10] You feel empowered to make a difference.

Invisible Children is tackling the issue of child soldiers in Uganda and Democratic Republic of Congo, among other worthy issues. This is a horrific epidemic throughout certain areas of Africa. The details are gruesome. But the organization chose to inspire us by putting the power to stop this epidemic in the hands of high schoolers and university students across the United States. The group's impact is nothing short of profound.

Too often we get so caught up in the immediate needs of people that we forget about the big picture. We've spent so much time guilting people into action that we've forgotten the power of inspiration. Inspired people get things done regardless of circumstances or lack of resources. Guilt fades, especially in the West.

Hollywood has motivated millions of people (myself included) to be more and do more because of the inspirational stories brought to the silver screen.

When I want people to do something, I spend about 20 percent of my time teaching them the methodology and 80 percent of my time inspiring them. Few forces are greater than a truly inspired individual.

What if we approached development work this way? What if we focused our efforts on inspiring the middle and upper classes to take care of their own people? This isn't a short-term solution or a substitute for emergency aid. I am merely suggesting an additional and simultaneous methodology.

What is more powerful? Westerners providing aid to Africa or inspired Africans elevating their own society to the point that they no longer need aid?

Start Something That Matters

Blake Mycoskie, founder of TOMS Shoes, knows that many of us are juggling these three questions:

1. Should I just focus on earning a living?
2. Should I pursue my passion and find work that I love?
3. Should I devote myself to a worthy cause that inspires me?

Fortunately for us, in his book *Start Something That Matters*, Blake tells us we don't have to choose.[11] As he shares the story of how he started TOMS, one of the fastest-growing shoe companies in the world, he says we'll have more success if we don't settle for less than combining all three elements.

I love his chapter titles— the six steps for creating your life:

1. Find your story.
2. Face your fears.
3. Be resourceful without resources.
4. Keep it simple.
5. Build trust.
6. Giving is good business.

His business model is this: "With every pair you purchase, TOMS will give a pair of shoes to a child in need." And he shows how doing something worthy, humanitarian, and godly can often be done better with a for-profit business. His principles confirm everything we teach at 48 Days and provide a very real example of someone who wouldn't settle for less than meaningful, purposeful, and profitable work.

I encourage you to pursue your passion, devote yourself to a worthy cause, and make a great living.

How does your work combine your passion, support a worthy cause, and provide extraordinary income?

Do you believe that's possible?

Do Good and Do Well

Change the world. Make some money. It's an appealing prospect. Nonprofits were created because for-profits weren't addressing some economic failures—pollution, poverty, and illiteracy. The best solution, however, may not be *either/or* but *and*. What if there were a way to create solutions for those failures and to generate reasonable profits for the organizers at the same time?

We've already mentioned terms like *social entrepreneurship* and *ethical capitalism*. Yes, there are new models for doing well while doing good. What I mean by that is that you can change the world, address pollution or poverty, share the gospel, make the world a better place—you get to decide what your passion is—*and make money* in the process.

I had the privilege of hearing John Sage describe his own interesting work history. John began his career at Microsoft, where he introduced Windows to the world. After that amazing success he registered for seminary but quickly realized he would be stifled in that environment. Instead, he recognized he could use his "capitalistic addiction" as his most effective tool for ministry and to create good in the world.

With a desire to help his college roommate in his efforts with the poor children of Peru, John and this roommate founded Pura Vida Coffee, where they sell fair trade, organic, shade-grown coffee.[12] Their philosophy is clear in their company motto: "It's better to give than receive. Unless you can do both."

The company has grown dramatically and is a great example of compassionate capitalism. Customers not only buy coffee but also ask how they can donate beyond the price of the coffee to participate in helping the children in the countries where the coffee is grown.

I love this growing awareness of social entrepreneurship or the understanding that we can shift capitalism to create good. Many of us come from backgrounds that make us question whether making money is somehow moving *away from* doing true ministry. *I am convinced it is the most effective and most direct path to actually increasing our ministry efforts.*

In his presentation John emphasized that we have to compete on quality and value to earn the right to ask people to support our causes. We can't offer shoddy service, sloppy necklaces, or second-rate coffee and expect people to get excited about helping us in our worthy endeavors. We have to be the very best. Then people will be proud to be a part of what's most important to us. Cutting-edge capitalism may be the best way for you to provide for your family and be a force for godly humanitarianism.

Jared and I consider ourselves social entrepreneurs. The task of a social entrepreneur is to recognize when a system or pattern of society is stuck in a self-defeating way. He or she finds what is not working and looks for innovative ways to reshape the negative system. We often hear that we should not just give a man a fish but teach him how to fish. Both of us are not content to just teach people how to find work; we are committed to revolutionizing our thinking about work.

Our traditional American concept of work is a striking example of a negative system. Our culture allows us to view work as a necessary evil or even a curse from God. Clichés like "Thank God It's Friday" and our eagerness for retirement convey our distaste for our daily work. Our goal, in the 48 Days community and in Jared's work around the world, is to show how work that is an authentic fit will do the following:

- Integrate your skills, personality traits, and passions.
- Provide a sense of meaning, accomplishment, and fulfillment.
- Be a person's greatest vehicle for living out God's purpose and calling.
- Ensure an unexpected flow of income and ultimate wealth.

> Money is a tool for proliferating love. It is not love itself, nor is it essential for life. It's a tool. When you understand money's role, it's easier to experience financial peace and view your work as a conduit for love, no matter the type of business or how you label it.
> —JARED ANGAZA

So You're Sayin' There's a Chance?

Okay, my tastes in movies are not very refined. I like funny and happy. Remember that great scene in *Dumb and Dumber* where Lloyd (Jim Carrey) and Harry (Jeff Daniels) have driven across the country to reconnect with Lloyd's dream girl, Mary (Lauren Holly)?[13] Lloyd asks about the chances that they could end up together. She replies, "Not good." As the scene unfolds Lloyd finds out his chances are like "one in a million."

But he's exuberant to find out there's a chance, albeit a slim one. His example makes me wonder how many times I've walked away from a dream because success was not guaranteed.

Would you continue toward your dream, knowing you had only one chance in a million? What were the chances that Jim Carrey would be paid $25 million for *Bruce Almighty* alone? What were the chances that a ninth-grade dropout would get any shot at making movies of any kind? It appears Jim Carrey is used to working toward the long shot.

As I've grown older I find more excitement in the ideas that are long shots. And, as in playing sports, gambling, inventing something, or writing popular books, the payoff is stupendous when the long shot comes in.

Are you pursuing any one-in-a-million ideas today? Or are you taking the safe route?

What are your ideas for making a difference in the world?

Do you have a plan for doing that without asking for donations?

How can your faith direct your creation of a for-profit ministry?

CHAPTER NINE

Retirement:
The American Dream?

Retirement is very much part of the American Dream. The clear model is to work because we have to, and then as soon as we've accumulated enough money to last for a few years, we can reward ourselves by quitting that stinking job and just doing nothing for the remainder of our days. Is that really the ideal?

When we talk about *retirement*, we typically mean when we stop working in something we don't enjoy. And then we fantasize about spending our time doing only things we do enjoy. When I get just enough money for my own needs, then I'll withdraw from anything that combines my passion, talent, and economic productivity.

Is that a reasonable way to refer to *retirement*? When can I stop this stupid job and start doing what I really enjoy? Do you really want to stop engaging in productive daily activities? Or to withdraw from service? Just take a quick trip to your local retirement center to see what happens to people who withdraw from active, meaningful service.

What Is Work?

We've already discussed work in previous chapters. But it's worth a recap: Is work the necessary evil that consumes the time between our brief periods of enjoyment on the weekend? Is it primarily a method of paying the bills and showing responsibility? A way to prove to our parents that the college degree was a reasonable investment? The shortest path to retirement? Or is it more than that?

The concepts of a fulfilling life are, for the most part, by-products of doing something we enjoy, with excellence, rather than things we can approach directly. Think for a moment about happiness, self-esteem, confidence, boldness, enthusiasm, fulfillment of calling and purpose, and money. These are not things we can approach directly; they are by-products of doing something we love and believe in. Then all those wonderful things sneak in the back door.

> Happiness is as a butterfly, which, when pursued, is always just beyond your grasp, but which, if you will sit down quietly, may alight upon you.
> —NATHANIEL HAWTHORNE[1]

In his popular book *The Millionaire Mind*, Thomas Stanley examines the characteristics of America's wealthiest people. He attempts to identify the distinguishing traits of those who ultimately become very wealthy. Is it IQ, GPA in school, college major, family opportunity, or type of business? Surprisingly none of these seem to be predictors of this extraordinary success. The one characteristic these people did have in common:

they were all doing something they loved. Dr. Stanley concludes, "If you love, absolutely love what you are doing, chances are excellent that you will succeed."[2]

Leo Tolstoy, struggling in his search for godliness, looked at the lives of his privileged class and the lives of the plain folks who were their laborers. He determined that whatever their hardships, the working folk were able to rest at night with basic peace and confidence in God's goodness, but the royals frequently complained and were unhappy about their lives. He renounced his wealthy class and set out to work in the fields alongside peasants. He proclaimed that the greatest error of the leisure class was the erroneous belief that "felicity consists in idleness." In *My Confession, My Religion* he asserted that we must return to the recognition "that work, and not idleness, is the indispensable condition of happiness for every human being."[3]

What if you were "allowed" to do what you most enjoyed every day? What would this do to the definition of *retirement*?

Do you know that in the Tibetan language there are no words for *unemployment* and *retirement*? These concepts are reserved for our Western culture where we have "jobs." In traditional Tibetan society, people were mostly farmers, animal herders, or merchants. There was no concept of setting hours of work or having a job. Their work was often seasonal, and during harvest season, they worked very hard. Then during the off-season, they and the land rested. With the dismantling of work models and the emphasis on work that is fulfilling, we are seeing the appeal of retirement diminishing as well.

That pattern of natural work and rest has been replaced in our culture with 24/7 accessibility to work. Cell phones ring in church, e-mail arrives at 2:00 a.m. demanding a response, and fax machines peel off pages of urgent business in family kitchens. We have created artificial environments with artificial work expectations.

We also attach a great deal of meaning to our jobs. Thus, if the job disappears, the immediate response can be that of diminished self-worth and clouded identity. A person without a job is assumed to have a life on hold. I have seen thousands of clients struggle with these inevitable transitions—hiding out to keep neighbors or friends from knowing the truth. If we have no identity apart from our jobs, we are truly vulnerable.

A gem cannot be polished without friction,
nor people perfected without trials.
—**CHINESE PROVERB**

I guess that's why I look back and value being raised on a farm where the sun and rain often dictated the day's activities. I love the convenience of modern technology, but as with all advancements there also comes the responsibility for maintaining personal life balance. Self-worth comes from meaningful time spent reading a good book, walking hand in hand with a spouse through a park, teaching a child to ride a bike, or volunteering for a Habitat for Humanity project.

I have always encouraged people to recognize times of being "between opportunities." Rather than feel the panic of being off-track, on hold, or unemployed, perhaps we should welcome such times as opportunities for new perspective, restoration, and rejuvenation.

What are three things that give you a sense of worth outside your job?

Don't Die Like This

Many people die with their music still in them. Why is this so? Too often it is because they are always getting ready to live. Before they know it, time runs out.

—OLIVER WENDELL HOLMES JR.[4]

Have you ever heard people brag about the wonderful things they are going to do . . .

- when the kids are grown?
- when they finally get a degree?
- when they get $1 million?
- when they get a promotion?
- when they retire?

Maybe those people are planning to travel more, write more, spend more time with family, or get in better health.

Have you also known someone who died before reaching that magic time in the future when "things" would be better? Of course you have. I have a friend who retired from a job he hated for many years. Can he now do all those things he's been dreaming of? No—his health is so poor from living an inauthentic life that he is essentially confined to his little house.

Are you waiting to start living your perfect life? Are you in danger of dying with your music still in you? What could you do today to release your music, even just a few bars?

Wisdom doesn't necessarily come with age.
Sometimes age just shows up all by itself.
—ZIGGY[5]

You're Never Too Old

There's a great story I love to tell about Grandma Moses, the renowned American folk artist. As a little girl she enjoyed painting and drawing and loved the involvement in art. People responded positively to the pieces she created. But as she came up through school, her well-meaning parents and teachers, who were people of influence in her life, said, "Well, that's fine that you enjoy painting, but you've got to do something to keep food on the table." The encouragement was to do something practical and realistic—something like typing and filing papers, which is exactly what she did.

She was able to get menial office jobs and eke out an existence. When she was sixty-seven years old, her husband died. She thought, *I'm an old woman. What do I want to do in my remaining years*? She remembered how much she had enjoyed painting and drawing as a little girl. She picked up painting again in order to create her postman's Christmas gift, saying it was easier to make a painting than to bake a cake over a hot stove.[6]

During the 1950s, Grandma Moses's exhibitions were so popular they broke attendance records all over the world. A cultural icon, the spry, productive, now elderly woman was continually cited as an inspiration for housewives, widows, and retirees. Her images of America's rural past were transferred to curtains, dresses, cookie jars, and dinnerware and used to pitch cigarettes, cameras, lipstick, and instant coffee.

In the next thirty years after her husband's death, she generated more than 3,600 canvases. She painted *Sugaring Off* when she was eighty-three, and it eventually sold for $1.2 million. A United States commemorative stamp was issued in her honor in 1969.

What a travesty to have a God-given gift pushed under the carpet because it wasn't practical or realistic. How would Grandma Moses's life have been changed if she had been encouraged to use her strongest God-given talents rather than those that were merely practical?

How would your life be different if you were using your strongest God-given talents?

What would your workweek be if you were working in your area of passion?

> What lies behind us and what lies before us are
> small matters compared to what lies within us.
> **—RALPH WALDO EMERSON**[7]

If I Had My Life to Live Over

I'd dare to make more mistakes next time.
    I'd relax, I would limber up.
I would be sillier than I have been this trip.
    I would take fewer things seriously.
I would take more chances.
I would climb more mountains and swim more rivers.
    I would eat more ice cream and less beans.
    I would perhaps have more actual troubles,
    but I'd have fewer imaginary ones.
You see, I'm one of those people who lived sensibly and
  sanely,
    hour after hour, day after day.
Oh, I've had my moments,
and if I had it to do over again,
    I'd have more of them.
In fact, I'd try to have nothing else.
    Just moments, one after another,
    instead of living so many years ahead of each day.
I've been one of those persons who never goes anywhere
    without a thermometer, a hot water bottle, a raincoat
      and a parachute.
If I had to do it again, I would travel lighter than I have.
If I had my life to live over,
    I would start barefoot earlier in the spring
    and stay that way later in the fall.
I would go to more dances.
    I would ride more merry-go-rounds.
    I would pick more daisies.[8]

Never Catch the Fox

I had the privilege recently of meeting with a distinguished businessman. And no, I didn't go to a nursing home to see this gentleman. This gentleman is now eighty-one years old, but he came to my office with a very big business proposal for a joint venture that would gain full benefit in the next three to five years. He had a spring in his step and a sparkle in his eyes, obviously enjoying every minute of our business discussion.

After I asked a little about his background, he shared that he had some early successes in business and retired to an island just off the East Coast a few years ago at the age of sixty-three. He achieved the success he was looking for and would never have to worry about money again. Then he told me, "Living on that island was the most miserable four years of my life." He returned to his roots in business and reengaged in the daily challenges that drove him previously.

His summary of what happened was simply, "Never catch the fox." What do the hounds do if they ever catch the fox, or what does a dog do if he actually catches the car? Watch them sit down and lose interest quickly.

Don't think reaching your goal is the only thrill. Understand that the process of getting there is actually more thrilling than arriving. I loved this man's gentle reminder to me not to just dream of the future but to savor today. Enjoy every step of your journey! And remember that success is not a destination; it's a direction.

Our life in Africa has almost nothing to do with the ideals of the current American Dream, which seems to be largely about collecting stuff and being normal. Clearly those aren't driving factors for us.

Our lives are centrally focused on relationships. Period. That's what drives us. That's what defines us. Our lives are designed around experiencing humanity and extending love by action and example. We have no desire to be normal or to operate within the status quo.

Since living in Africa I've experienced more of humanity than ever before. On any given day I will interact with a minimum of six to ten ethnicities, religions, and cultures. I love the life and wisdom that this eclectic cocktail of humanity breathes into our lives.

Our stuff is minimal. Our house is basic. We don't have many things. We live in Africa. We interact with a plethora of cultures. We crave human interaction and story, not mass conformity or normalcy. We don't have all sorts of insurance coverage or a 401(k) or a mortgage. And we intend to live and raise our family in a developing nation—in Africa or otherwise—not in the comfort of America.

Frankly we like being what others would define as *weird*. I'm fully aware that we are far outside the norm and far outside what has been defined as *the American Dream*.

But I'm noticing a shift in American society, in both the young and young at heart. Age doesn't seem to be as much of a factor now. In all walks of life—from the high school kid who will build the next Facebook craze to the grandfather realizing he has not yet lived—people are realizing that the old American Dream is dying.

Our attention as a society is shifting back toward human connection. Businesses are becoming more socially conscious and ecologically responsible, and even technology is being used to bring people closer together. The world is becoming smaller every day with our easy access to affordable travel and communication.

The goals of holding a job for thirty years and getting your gold watch when you retire are becoming ancient relics. Life isn't just about having a steady job, house, and car and keeping up with the Joneses anymore. Sure, that model still represents the majority, but a growing revolution of people out there has replaced those priorities with those of human connection, relationship, and purpose.

I don't believe that we, as a society, will ever come to a place where we tolerate the exploitation of people and the earth for the purpose of mass consumption again. We know too much now, and information flows too freely. The Internet has created a level of transparency that previously did not exist. It has created awareness and the ability to influence and incite change. We are in the midst of a true revolution.

Here in Mombasa, I am on a never-ending adventure. I've sort of set myself up to never be able to "catch the fox" because there is always a new, more agile fox coming into the picture. Yes, we have serious difficulties, and we see atrocities daily. But it's raw and real. It's no ordinary life. And ultimately I don't want to catch the fox. I just want to continually find new and more challenging foxes to chase. It's the chase that refines and often defines us.

Society, now more than ever, is beginning to realize that life is about more than achieving business conquests and accumulating stuff. Life is much more about embracing the journey and much less about reaching the destination. We're learning to appreciate and live in the now. And most important, we're learning that there is no substitute for human connection.

How Will You Be Remembered?

At his ninetieth birthday party, Little Jimmy Dickens was asked what he wanted his legacy to be. Now here's a guy who could brag about being the shortest country singer (four feet, eleven inches), the flashiest, or the oldest living member of the Grand Ole Opry. Or he could wish that he would be remembered for his biggest hits, including such classics as "May the Bird of Paradise Fly Up Your Nose," "(I Got a) Hole in My Pocket," "Take an Old Cold Tater (and Wait)," and "When the Ship Hit the Sand."

And while I know each of you would love to have that notoriety, that's not what Little Jimmy said he wanted to be remembered for. He said, "I've been honest with people," and a friend at the event pointed out that Little Jimmy was a kind man.[9] It appears a great legacy doesn't require fame, fortune, or memorable lyrics. Being honest and kind is something we can all choose to leave as a lasting legacy to those who know us best.

> Treat every person with kindness and respect, even those who are rude to you. Remember that you show compassion to others not because of who they are but because of who you are.
> —ANDREW T. SOMERS[10]

Work Six Weeks a Year—That's All

Is getting more stuff always a reasonable goal?

Henry David Thoreau spent the better part of his life writing about man's attempt to find truth and meaning through simplified living. At some point he discovered he could live within the harmony and beauty of nature with a clear conscience and work only six weeks a year to support his lifestyle.

Finding a teaching job that matched his style proved difficult, so Henry worked briefly in his father's pencil factory. At age twenty-eight, he built a small house on Walden Pond and began to devote his time to his writing. Advocating the simple life, he began his Walden journey with these words: "I went to the woods because I wished to live deliberately."[11]

His words do not describe the typical journey of a college graduate today. Rather, the expectation is an immediate six-figure income and the lifestyle that accompanies success. We live in a society that embraces indulgent consumption as a visible status symbol. The fabulous house tells everyone you have arrived, even if it takes having two incomes and being trapped in an unfulfilling job to make it work. The house then sets the expectations for the country club membership, private schools for the children, and attendance at the right social events. We work longer hours to pay for the new stuff and then have less time to enjoy it. We plead with God to bless us, but the only relief from the self-imposed pressure would be to win the lottery.

Where do we draw the line on consumption if we can *afford* the extras? Do you really need all the house you qualify for? Should we really thank God for providing when we finance a car purchase equal to an annual income? Is taking a vacation in the Caribbean that much more satisfying than spending a week on a needy Native American reservation? Is it truly God's will that we buy into the bondage of debt? How can we give generously when payments are overdue?

Perhaps we, like Thoreau, could take time to savor the beauty of nature around us and to smell the fresh roses of everyday life. He wrote,

I went to the woods because I wished to live deliberately, to front only the essential facts of life, and see if I could not learn what it had to teach, and not, when I came to die, discover that I had not lived. I did not wish to live what was not life, living is so dear; nor did I wish to practise [*sic*] resignation, unless it was quite necessary. I wanted to live deep and suck out all the marrow of life, to live so sturdily and Spartan-like as to put to rout all that was not life, to cut a broad swath and shave close, to drive life into a corner, and reduce it to its lowest terms, and, if it proved to be mean, why then to get the whole and genuine meanness of it, and publish its meanness to the world; or if it were sublime, to know it by experience, and be able to give a true account of it in my next excursion. For most men, it appears to me, are in a strange uncertainty about it, whether it is of the devil or of God, and have *somewhat hastily* concluded that it is the chief end of man here to "glorify God and enjoy him forever." . . . Simplify, simplify.[12]

What would your life look like if you really lived a simple life? Are you currently sucking all the marrow out of life?

One should never count the years—one should instead count one's interests. I have kept young trying never to lose my childhood sense of wonderment. I am glad I still have a vivid curiosity about the world I live in.
—HELEN KELLER[13]

CHAPTER TEN

I Have a Feeling We're Not in Kansas Anymore

The workplace has changed and will never be the same again. We can fight the survival struggles of the auto industry, the formerly accepted banking practices, the correction in real estate values, and the traditional employee expectations, but we can never return to the life of even ten years ago. We cannot stop change. We can only choose how we will respond to change and in choosing decide whether it is good or bad. And our decisions will determine whether we are moving in positive or negative directions. We can agree that not all change is good, but we can also agree that by definition all progress requires change. So let's stay open to the possibility that change—even if unwelcomed and unexpected—could open the door to unanticipated progress.

There is nothing either good or bad,
but thinking makes it so.
—WILLIAM SHAKESPEARE[1]

Outta Work but Finding Life

A couple of years ago I offered a little contest for my newsletter readers about being out of work. I asked them if they were out of work to send a brief note to me explaining how they lost their job and what they were moving toward. About ten minutes after the newsletter went out, the messages started rolling in. While many were very sad and disheartening, I was also thrilled to see the optimism sneak in, even for those who were still in the process of clarifying the next step. Here are just a few snippets:

- "From now on I am moving toward listening to my heart and soul."
- "At first I was stunned, then upset, and then I thought, wait a minute . . . this is really a blessing."
- "I am so excited about the happy and prosperous times ahead for this year. Life Is Good!"
- "This 'in-between' time has given me the opportunity to get started with launching an independent training and career coaching practice, which has been a dream of mine."
- "I was a journalist for ten years and was laid off. But that's okay. It's truly turned into a great period of refreshment in my life."
- "I had secretly wished that I would be the one to be released, but when it happened, I was still shocked. I recognized that we're in the middle of a recession, but this was the kind of situation that always happened to someone else . . . not me. While it sounds cliché, this was truly a blessing."

- "I was laid off on March 9, with no warning after working for a major manufacturer for eleven and half years. When I told my wife, her response was, 'Good. Now you can go and do something you want to do.'"
- "I had a great interview today and another interview with a different company tomorrow that looks like it could be my dream job—onward and upward!"
- "At first the loss of my job was very unsettling; however, in time I have come to believe that this is God's way of getting me on to something bigger and better."
- "I was a little surprised that they beat me to the punch, but I thanked them saying, 'I really appreciate this, I really do.'"

It's clear that change, even if unexpected and unwelcomed, can lead to better and more fulfilling work in the future.

Honey, I Got Fired

Nathaniel Hawthorne went home to tell his wife that he had just been fired from his job.

"Good," she said. "Now you can write your book."

"What do we live on meanwhile?" Hawthorne asked.

His wife opened a drawer filled with money. "I have always known that you are a man of genius," she said. "So I saved a little each week, and now I have enough to last for a year." Hawthorne used the time to write *The Scarlet Letter*, one of the masterpieces of American literature.[2]

Failure is simply the opportunity to begin
again, this time more intelligently.
—HENRY FORD[3]

Reverse Telecommuting

There are so many new words being birthed by the changing
workplace. Words like *googling* as a verb, *electronic immigrants,*
prairie dogging, ohnosecond, blamestorming, seagull manager,
chainsaw consultant, flight risk, uninstalled, and *cube farm.*

We all understand the term *telecommuting*: when you have
work from the office to complete at home. How about the opposite of that: *reverse telecommuting*? This is the commonplace
practice of bringing personal work to the office. It's no secret that
employees spend a whole lot of time paying personal bills, making personal phone calls, making flight arrangements or medical
and social appointments, reading online newspapers, updating
Facebook, and texting family members—all on company time.

Arguably some of these things can be handled only during
normal work hours, but how much is acceptable? According to
a survey by America Online and Salary.com, the average worker
admits to frittering away 2.09 hours per eight-hour workday,
not including lunch and scheduled break times.[4] Yes, companies
assume a certain amount of wasted time when they determine
employee pay. However, the survey indicates employees are wast-
ing about twice as much time as their employers expect. Estimates
are that employers are spending $759 billion per year on salaries
for which real work was expected but not actually performed.[5]

Would you be willing to be paid for results only rather than for time spent in the office? Would that increase or decrease your compensation?

No Cubicle—No Problem

The number of people who are self-employed or work from home is growing exponentially. Using figures from the IRS, the Bureau of Labor Statistics, the Small Business Administration, and the National Federation of Independent Business, it appears the number is somewhere around thirty million in the United States alone. Whatever the number, we know the attraction for both companies and workers is growing as well.[6] Sun Microsystems calculates that it saved $400 million over six years in real estate costs alone by allowing nearly half of its employees to work anywhere they want.[7] At IBM 40 percent of the workforce has no official office.[8] At AT&T a third of the managers can work from anywhere they choose.[9] If you make a reservation with JetBlue Airways, you are talking with an agent who is working from home.[10]

Everyone benefits from a distributed worker model for these reasons:

- Companies save on rent and utilities.
- Workers save on gas, wardrobes, and eating out.
- Distributed workers are *more* productive.
- Time becomes less important; results matter.
- With increased freedom, workers can have a life.

Maybe you could *increase* your opportunities for fulfilling and profitable work by suggesting that you would be willing to work from home. You don't need the company to supply a computer, a telephone, a wastebasket, a file cabinet, cheap wall decorations, a bookcase, a cubicle, or a water cooler.

Successful work models are changing every day. Release your creativity to imagine a work model that provides unique value for an organization and for you. Then share that model with thirty to forty companies. You will find a match.

On Your Own but Not Alone

Ever find yourself trying to be an entrepreneur but also trying to escape from the kids or being distracted by the unpredictable noise around your table at Starbucks? You might want to try *coworking*.

One of the hot new terms accounting for people wanting to work not from home and not from an office is *coworking*. People who struggle with watching *Seinfeld* reruns or playing Xbox in the middle of the afternoon may find that a shared office space is just what they need.

The term just made it into Wikipedia and is defined thus: "Coworking is the social gathering of a group of people, who are still working independently, but who share values and who are interested in the synergy that can happen from working with talented people in the same space."[11] Blogs, social networks, and other support systems are being formed around this concept.

Sole proprietors, freelancers, artists, consultants, and other independent workers are finding refuge in coworking environments with open office areas but dedicated work space, high-speed Internet, a kitchenette, and maybe even a printer and a fax machine. Rates range from fifteen dollars a day to five hundred dollars a month for full twenty-four-hour access. Check it out at CoWorking Spaces[12] or just google your city with the word *coworking*.

Why Turkeys Get "Benefits"—and the Axe

Once upon a time long, long ago, the Eagle and the Turkey were very good friends. Everywhere they went these friends went together. It was not uncommon for people to look up and see the Eagle and the Turkey flying side by side through the air.

One day while flying, the Turkey said to the Eagle: "Let's drop down and get a bite to eat. My stomach is growling."

"Sounds like a good idea to me," replied the Eagle. So the two birds glided down to earth, saw several animals eating, and decided to join them. They landed next to the Cow. The Cow was busy eating corn, but noticed that the Eagle and the Turkey were soon sitting on the ground next to her.

"Welcome," said the Cow. "Help yourself to the corn."

This took the two birds by surprise. They were not accustomed to having other animals share their food quite so readily.

"Why are you willing to share your corn with us?" asked the Eagle.

"Oh, we have plenty to eat here. Mr. Farmer gives us all we want," replied the Cow. With that invitation, the Eagle and the Turkey jumped in and ate their fill. When they finished, the Turkey asked more about Mr. Farmer. "Well," said the Cow, "he grows all our food. We don't have to work for the food at all."

"You mean," said the Turkey, "that Mr. Farmer simply gives you all you want to eat?"

"That's right," said the Cow. "Not only that, but he gives us a place to live."

The Turkey and the Eagle were shocked! They had never heard of such a thing. They had always had to search for food and work for shelter.

When it came time to leave, the Turkey and the Eagle began to discuss the situation. "Maybe we should just stay here," said the Turkey. "We can have all the food we want without working. And that barn over there sure beats those nests we have been building. Besides, I'm getting tired of always having to work for a living."

"I don't know about all this," said the Eagle. "It sounds too good to be true. I find it hard to believe that one can get something for nothing. Besides, I kinda like flying high and free through the air. And providing for food and shelter isn't so bad. In fact, I find it quite challenging."

Well, the Turkey thought it over and decided to stay where there was free food and shelter. But the Eagle decided that he loved his freedom too much to give it up and enjoyed the consistent challenge of making his own living. So, after saying good-bye to his old friend the Turkey, the Eagle set sail for the unknown adventure.

Everything went fine for the Turkey. He ate all he wanted. He never worked. He grew fat and lazy. But then one day he heard the farmer's wife mention that Thanksgiving was coming in the next few days and it would be nice to have roast turkey for dinner. Hearing that, the Turkey decided it was time to check out and rejoin his good friend Mr. Eagle. But when he attempted to fly he found that he had grown too fat and lazy. Instead of being able to fly, he could only flutter. So on Thanksgiving Day the farmer's family sat down to roast Turkey.[13]

We are completing several years of bailouts, extended benefits, and expectations of being "taken care of." *When you give up the challenges of life in pursuit of security, you may give up your freedom.*

Need a new map for your life?

In his book *A Whack on the Side of the Head*, Roger von Oech tells a story about a Native American medicine man. Whenever the tribe was having difficulty finding game, the medicine man would take a dried animal skin, crinkle it repeatedly until deep lines appeared, and then mark it with some places already familiar to the hunters. Then he would tell the hunting party that it was an ancient map and that the crinkled lines showed the best hunting trails used by their ancestors. Armed with this new information, the hunting party set out with confidence and enthusiasm, and surprisingly enough, they always found an abundance of game for the tribe.[14]

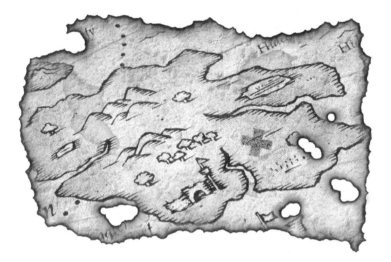

The map was nothing but randomly created lines. So why did it unleash new success for the hunters? I think we can see several reasons:

- It broke the rut of sameness.
- It encouraged them to look in places nearby but off the familiar path.
- It produced a positive anticipation.
- It put the tools for success in their hands—no excuses, no blaming.
- It was presented as a hidden secret.

Having trouble finding "game"? Why don't you get a new map? (At this point in my writing, I actually took a blank piece of paper, crumpled it up, then opened it again. I imagined my house and saw the familiar roads. But then I was amazed at what I began to see.)

What if you just made a new map? Start to see where it could lead you.

Winners Never Quit—Baloney!

We've all heard the old adage, "Winners never quit; quitters never win." Is that really true? Does that mean that if you're driving from Detroit to Miami and you suddenly realize you're actually headed for Savannah, you would simply continue driving? Or even speed up? Or just try harder? Of course not. You would immediately correct your direction, even if it meant going back to Atlanta to get on the right road.

Why is it that in jobs or businesses people often believe that if they just persist, somehow things will get better? And that they need to be loyal and never show signs of giving up?

Here's a question from a female listener of my podcast: "I would like to know what to do when you are working so hard and everything seems to continue to fail. Do you change plans or what?"

And here's my response: Quitting a job does not mean that you're quitting your commitment to provide for your family. Quitting a business does not mean that you are walking away from the thrill of controlling your time and income. Quitting a ministry or nonprofit organization does not mean that you've given up on your desire to change the world or help the less fortunate.

Your job, business, or ministry is just one strategy to accomplish your bigger vision. Your purpose or calling defines the big goal. If your job is clearly a dead end, it makes perfect sense to quit, take your skills to a better work environment, and release your ability to provide for your family. If your business is failing, learn from the experience and start in a new direction. I constantly have areas in my business and personal life that are on the bubble. If they are not proven successful in a very specific period of time, they're gone. I quit but keep moving on to success in other ways.

Here are my recommendations:

- If your job provides nothing for you but a meager paycheck, plan to quit and be gone in the next thirty days.
- If you have been running your business for one year and after expenses it's only netting you five hundred dollars a month, quit and find a new venture.
- If you started a nonprofit ministry and after two years you find that you are spending 80 percent of your time on administrative work and have no real economic model for continuing, consider linking arms with an established organization.

Winners quit. They quit quickly and often. Yes, I know we hear that "nothing matters but persistence," but if you are a duck trying to climb a tree, all persistence will get you is webbed feet that are too sore to even swim well. Have the maturity and guts to *quit* the ineffective things in your life.

While we're at it, ask yourself whether these well-known adages are always true:

1. The customer is always right.
2. Everything happens for a reason.
3. Never judge a book by its cover.
4. You can't teach an old dog new tricks.
5. Absence makes the heart grow fonder.
6. Better be safe than sorry.
7. Good fences make good neighbors.
8. You can't have your cake and eat it too.

Don't let commonly accepted clichés misdirect you from the unique path you are on. There are many exceptions to each of these time-honored clichés.

ADVANCING IN ANOTHER DIRECTION

There are thousands of mission programs, aid agencies, and goodwilled philanthropists in the world today. Altruism has been with us since the beginning of time, and I'm grateful for that. Unfortunately a lot of the methodology used today also seems to be from the beginning of time.

Civilizations change drastically over time. Our methods of altruism should adapt appropriately. What helped before may no longer be helpful or relevant now. A commitment to adaptability is absolutely crucial in order to truly be effective and create a positive impact.

The business world is constantly adapting to the needs and desires of customers. Why is this not the ongoing model of philanthropy? Broken, antiquated systems plug along year after year, often causing more damage than good. Donors continue funding them because they are equally out of touch with the intended beneficiaries.

Aid agencies are often built on systems that foster donor dependency. They don't adapt because they risk losing their funding. They need funding, so they develop a simple mission designed to compel, if not appease, donors. Those donors then insist the agency continue on that path, despite the need for adaptation.

Many philanthropists, aid agencies, and other altruistic entities have convinced themselves that winners never quit. They proudly march on, carrying out the same strategy that they had sometimes decades earlier. They set out to achieve something, and by whatever means, they are going to achieve it.

But they fail to realize you must adapt your strategy as you go, and often that means you must change the methodology entirely. People change. Environments change. Priorities change. These things happen daily. Consequently, aid programs and social enterprises must adapt quickly and often in order to serve the needs of the people.

Many companies have grown so accustomed to just plugging away at the same strategy that they've created a monster. Adapting is a bit like turning the *Titanic* around. It's too big a machine with too many moving parts. It's easier to steady the course and not rock the boat, so to speak.

General Douglas MacArthur is famously quoted to have said, "We are not retreating; we are advancing in another direction." This doesn't change the goal, just the methodology. It doesn't represent a failure. It represents a true commitment to and relationship with the people you serve.

If you're committed to serving the people, not the system, it is always going to be necessary to adapt and advance in another direction when your methods are no longer serving the people's needs. It's your duty as a philanthropist to stay in tune with the people enough to know when this need arises.

Put In 10,000 Hours—Then We'll Talk

I frequently encounter employees who want a guaranteed salary before they show up the first day, musicians who want to be signed before they've proven their talent, house cleaners who want to be paid even if not needed, celebrities who expect a meaningful marriage after a three-day romance, and authors who want my endorsement for their book but don't want to give me a copy to read.

Have we forgotten that to reap a harvest of corn you have to first plant seeds, and to receive warmth from a stove you must first put in wood?

Charles Dickens wrote stories for a London magazine for almost three years with no payment.[15] Much to his surprise and delight, he was then approached by a young publisher who wanted to collect his writings into a volume along with ten prints from an illustrator. That success led to *The Pickwick Papers* and made him the most popular author in the world at that time (1836). Over the next twenty years, more than 1.6 million copies of *Pickwick* were sold.[16]

Joanne and I taught a free weekly seminar called CareerLink for more than eight years, simply encouraging people and giving them our copies of information that would help them, before the "overnight" success of *48 Days to the Work You Love*.

In *Outliers* Malcolm Gladwell says that people who attain extraordinary success put in 10,000 hours before reaching their success.[17] Today too many people are expecting a shortcut to fame and fortune.

What are you doing to put in your 10,000 hours toward the dream you know is coming?[18]

Your ability to blend wisdom with passion will open the doors for you—equipping you to accomplish your greatest financial goals, experience the thrill of fulfilling relationships, create meaningful work, and complete your purpose and calling here on earth in your unique way. Enjoy the process.

Acknowledgments

We extend our thanks to the wisdom and passion influences in our lives:

To the mentors who opened my eyes to possibilities beyond the farm fields in Ohio. I wish to thank Earl Nightingale, Brian Tracy, Denis Waitley, Norman Vincent Peale, Dale Carnegie, David Schwartz, Stephen Covey, and many more whom I never met in person, yet their messages shaped the life of a kid whose future looked predictably small.

I offer my gratitude to Zig Ziglar, whose kindness and authenticity have served as a guiding light for many years. His model of serving others helped confirm that the success of those around me could enhance my own. His materials were constants in our home, as evidenced by those stories being told by my children to my grandchildren.

Mark Victor Hansen, with his early MEGA Book Marketing University, showed me the importance of *selling* well along with *writing* well in the process of becoming a well-known author.

To all my current writing friends, including Dave Ramsey, Ken Abraham, Dan Scott, and Andy Andrews, I express my gratitude for your openness and the encouragement to live and write as evidence of being fully alive.

To the many students, clients, readers, and friends who have shared their struggles and triumphs so freely, I submit my thanks and gratitude. Many of those stories are reflected here in more than subtle ways. The favor I now have as an author, speaker, and coach has been developed only as a result of your willingness to be transparent as we learned the lessons of life together.

I wish to express my thanks to Matt Baugher and the entire team at Thomas Nelson. Matt became a friend first, long before the relationship I now have with him as my publisher. He brings a vast knowledge of the publishing industry to the table—both where it has come from and where it is going. His inspiration and excitement about the changes are refreshing in an industry that frequently conveys dread and fear to authors.

And of course to Joanne, my wife and biggest fan since I was just a teenager, I offer gratefulness that goes beyond description. Thanks for your unwavering support and encouragement for me to make a way, even if there was no path.

—Dan Miller

First and foremost, I thank my father, Dan, for always encouraging me to dream big and believe in myself. He encouraged me in the way I was bent and constantly fostered my creativity and uniqueness. He and my grandfather, Ray Miller, instilled in me the incredible work ethic of the Amish, and for that, I am eternally grateful.

Thank you, Mom, for exemplifying love and creating a haven of peace in our family. That understanding of love has provided a solid foundation for the passion that drives me not just to do more but to be more. My love for humanity started with you.

Thank you, Mom and Dad, for instilling in me a true sense

of purpose and an insatiable thirst for the extraordinary. You are my biggest inspirations.

Thank you to my incredible, beautiful wife, Ilea. You continually inspire me to be a better man. Your love gives me strength. Your wisdom challenges me. *Nakupenda milele.*

To the change makers out there who have inspired and educated me. I grew up listening to Zig Ziglar, Brian Tracy, Michael Gerber, Tony Robbins, and a plethora of others. I am so grateful to have been blessed with the teachings of these great men at such an early age. (And thank you, Dad, for giving me the gift of knowledge instead of mindless TV. Now I understand.)

To Seth Godin, for guiding me through his books. He exemplifies extraordinary. He's our real-life Willy Wonka, always daring to dream bigger and to bring those dreams into fruition. You taught me to never settle for anything less than extraordinary. Most important, you taught me to ship. You are truly an extraordinary man. Thank you for your art.

Thank you, Dad and Matt Baugher, for affording me the opportunity to contribute to this book. It is an honor and a privilege to work with you both.

—Jared Angaza

Notes

Chapter One: I Just Want to Make a Difference

1. As quoted in Jack Canfield and Kent Healy, *The Success Principles for Teens: How to Get from Where You Are to Where You Want to Be* (Deerfield Beach, FL: Health Communications, 2008), 47.
2. Dan Allender, *Sabbath* (Nashville: Thomas Nelson, 2009), 190.
3. Maggie Gobran (lecture, Global Leadership Summit, South Barrington, IL, 12 August 2011), http://www.jennicatron.tv /global-leadership-summit-mama-maggie.
4. http://www.somaly.org/about-smf/somaly-mam.
5. Richard Langworth, ed., *Churchill by Himself: The Definitive Collection of Quotations* (New York: Public Affairs, 2011), 594.
6. Tom Van Riper, "First Job: Donald Trump," Forbes.com, 23 May 2006, http://www.forbes.com/2006/05/20/donald-trump-jobs _cx_tr_06work_0523trump.html.
7. Marc Benioff and Carlye Adler, *The Business of Changing the World: Twenty Great Leaders on Strategic Corporate Philanthropy* (New York: McGraw-Hill, 2007), 53.
8. Staff, "Celebrity First Jobs," Forbes.com, 11 May 2007, http://www .msnbc.msn.com/id/18577825/ns/business-forbes_com /t/celebrity-first-jobs/#.T19iQq49hN4; Dorothy Pomerantz, "Hollywood's Highest-Earning Actors," Forbes.com, 1 August 2011,

http://www.forbes.com/sites/dorothypomerantz/2011/08/01
/hollywoods-highest-earning-actors.

9. Staff, "Celebrity First Jobs," Forbes.com, 11 May 2007, http://
www.msnbc.msn.com/id/18577825/ns/business-forbes_com/t
/celebrity-first-jobs/#.T19iQq49hN4.

10. Stefan Kanfer, *Ball of Fire: The Tumultous Life and Comic Art of
Lucille Ball* (New York: Random House, 2003), 29.

11. Roger Moore, "Tom Hanks Wants to Spread Optimism with His
New Movie 'Larry Crowne,'" *Orlando Sentinel*, 24 June 2011.

12. Emily-Fortune Feimster, "Madonna the Donut Girl?: A Labor
Day Look at Stars' Pre-fame Jobs," Beck/Smith Hollywood,
http://becksmithhollywood.com/?p=2560. In June 2010,
Madonna was listed tenth on the Celebrity 100 list by Forbes.
com. The list ranks the richest and most powerful actors,
actresses, and musicians, http://www.forbes.com/2010/06/22
/lady-gaga-oprah-winfrey-business-entertainment-celeb-100-10
_land.html?partner=blogsceleb100. Such rankings usually
change each year, depending on celebrities' earnings.

13. Ibid.

14. Maria Carey biography, http://www.imdb.com/name
/nm0001014/bio; Kate Lorenz, "First Jobs of the Rich and
Famous," Careerbuilder.com, http://www.careerbuilder.com
/Article/CB-571-Job-Search-Strategies-First-Jobs-of-the-Rich
-and-Famous.

15. Angelina Jolie biography, http://www.thebiographychannel
.co.uk/biographies/angelina-jolie.html.

16. Bono biography, http://www.thebiographychannel.co.uk
/biographies/bono.html.

17. George Clooney biography, http://www.thebiographychannel
.co.uk/biographies/george-clooney. html; http://www
.satsentinel.org.

18. http://www.unhcr.org/cgi-bin/texis/vtx/home. UNHCR
refers to the Office of the United Nations High Commissioner
for Refugees. "Angelina Jolie and Brad Pitt Give Millions to
Charities," Hollywire.com, 22 March 2008, http://www
.hollywire.com/the-news-dump
/angelina-jolie-and-brad-pitt-give-millions-to-charities.

19. "Perry Farrell Charity Work, Events, and Causes," Look to the
Stars, http://www.looktothestars.org/celebrity/475-perry-farrell;
http://www.virginrecords.com/perry.

20. Editors, "AfriGadget: Using African Ingenuity to Solve Everyday Problems," Odewire, 23 December 2008, http://odewire .com/?s=afrigadget; http://www.afrigadget.com.

21. Official site of Mark Twain, http://www.cmgww.com/historic /twain/about/index.php.

22. Frederick Buechner, a graduation address, as quoted in Ken Gire, *Windows of the Soul* (Grand Rapids, MI: Zondervan, 1996), 71.

23. Thomas Merton, *New Seeds of Contemplation* (New York: New Directions, 2007), 29.

24. http://www.48days.com/coaching.

25. Norman Vincent Peale, *The Positive Power of Jesus Christ* (Carmel, NY: Guideposts, 1980), 87.

26. T. Harv Eker, *Secrets of the Millionaire Mind* (New York: HarperCollins, 2005), 10.

27. http://www.thefreedictionary.com/doofus.

28. "Pope John XXIII," *Telegraph* (UK), 14 September 2005.

29. http://normanvincentpeale.wwwhubs.com.

30. Zig Ziglar, *See You at the Top* (Gretna, LA: Pelican, 2000), 150.

31. http://www.48days.com/coaching/coaches.

32. http://www.48days.com/48businessideas.

33. http://www.davidfoster.com; "Hitman: David Foster and Friends," PBS, http://www.pbs.org/wnet/gperf/episodes /hitman-david-foster-friends/introduction/456.

34. Thomas Stanley, *The Millionaire Mind* (Kansas City, MO: Andrews McMeel, 2001), 13.

35. Lizzie James, "Interview with Jim Morrison," http://www .cinetropic.com/morrison/james.html.

36. Henry David Thoreau, *Walden: or, Life in the Woods* (Boston: Houghton Mifflin, 1893), 498–99, http://books.google.com /books?id=ia_NRtTcT74C&q=if+one+advances+#v=onepage& q=if%20one%20advances&f=false.

37. Sir Edward Gibbon, *The History of the Decline and Fall of the Roman Empire*, vol. 1 (1782), 133, http://books.google .com/books?id=gRE0q38Nb70C&pg=PA133&lpg=PA133&dq=f ire+of+genius+extinguished&source=bl&ots=v _KPm4ekpE&sig=SgTtsZZbBzlh_Rs6fBwfkGw6UOU&hl=en& ei=ziwKTarJBsP6lwfAh5G4Aw&sa=X&oi=book_result&ct=res ult&resnum=9&sqi=2&ved=0CGMQ6AEwCA#v=onepage&q= fire%20of%20genius%20extinguished&f=false.

38. Adam Smith, *The Wealth of Nations* (Blacksburg, VA: Thrifty Books, 2009), 560.

Chapter Two: Where Do I Find Security?

1. http://jaredmiller.tumblr.com/post/1250437573/we-can-all -live-in-wonderland.
2. http://www.ratm.com.
3. www.coldplay.com.
4. Blake Ellis, "Average Student Loan Debt Tops $25,000," CNNMoney, 3 November 2011, http://money.cnn .com/2011/11/03/pf/student_loan_debt/index.htm. The average debt for four years of college depends on the school and the state: "Debt loads varied dramatically depending on the state— anywhere from an average of $15,500 in Utah to $31,050 in New Hampshire. Not so surprisingly, the ranges were even more dramatic on the school level, with average debts ranging from $950 to $55,250."
5. Henry David Thoreau, *Walden: or, Life in the Woods* (Boston: Houghton Mifflin, 1893), 143, http://books.google.com /books?id=ia_NRtTcT74C&printsec=frontcover#v=onepage&q =live%20deep&f=false.
6. Address to the United Nations, 25 September 1961, http:// www.jfklibrary.org/Research/Ready-Reference/JFK-Speeches /Address-Before-the-General-Assembly-of-the-United-Nations -September-25-1961.aspx.
7. Wayne Dyer, *Your Erroneous Zones* (New York: Avon Books, 1995), 141.
8. As quoted in Harold Kent Straughn, *LifeSpirals* (St. Louis, MO: Chalice Press, 2009), 184.
9. Samuel Brannan, "Founder of the Fireman's Fund," *The Standard: A Weekly Insurance Newspaper*, vol. 87, 27 November 1920, 654, http://books.google.com/books?id=gI3nAAAAMAA J&dq=samuel+brannan+store&q=brannan#v=snippet&q=bra nnan&f=false. To compute the difference in dollars from 1848 to the present, go to http://www.measuringworth.com/uscompare /relativevalue.php.
10. http://www.panicbuttons.com.
11. http://www.anthologygearwear.com.
12. http://customstix.com/info.

13. http://www.chadjeffers.com/25-notes.
14. See Daniel H. Pink, *Free Agent Nation: The Future of Working for Yourself* (New York: Warner Books, 2001), http://astore.amazon.com/48days0b-20/detail/0446678791.
15. Bureau of Labor Statistics, National Longitudinal Studies, http://www.bls.gov/nls/nlsfaqs.htm#anch4.
16. As quoted in Jeffrey D. Schultz and Luchen Li, *Critical Companion to John Steinbeck* (New York: Facts on File, 2005), 142. They noted these words came from Steinbeck's "More about Aristocracy," *Saturday Review*, 10 December 1955.
17. As quoted in William F. Buckley Jr., *Up from Liberalism* (New Rochelle, NY: Arlington House, 1968), 174.
18. The Social Security Act of 1935: "On August 14, 1935, the Social Security Act established a system of old-age benefits for workers, benefits for victims of industrial accidents, unemployment insurance, aid for dependent mothers and children, the blind, and the physically handicapped," http://www.ourdocuments.gov/doc.php?flash=true&doc=68. Gene Smiley, "Great Depression," *Concise Encyclopedia of Economics*, http://www.econlib.org/library/Enc/GreatDepression.html.
19. Dambisa Moyo, "Why Foreign Aid Is Hurting Africa," *Wall Street Journal*, 21 March 2009, http://online.wsj.com/article/SB123758895999200083.html.
20. Famous Quotes, SABC (a broadcasting firm), 14 June 2011, http://www.sabc.co.za/mandela/featuredetails/923ec4004739b9f792a89bac2f00ab93/group1.
21. "Inspirational Quotes," Nordskog Publishing, http://www.nordskogpublishing.com/presidential_quotes.shtml.
22. Live interview with Charlie Rose, 12 December 2007, http://www.charlierose.com/view/interview/8831.
23. "What Is Your Life's Blueprint?" http://seattletimes.nwsource.com/special/mlk/king/words/blueprint.html. Six months before he was assassinated, King spoke to a group of students at Barratt Junior High School in Philadelphia, 26 October 1967.
24. Dan Miller, *48 Days to the Work You Love*, rev. ed. (Nashville: B&H Publishing Group, 2010), http://www.48days.com/store.
25. John Maxwell, *Talent Is Never Enough* (Nashville: Thomas Nelson, 2007), 9.
26. Eleanor Roosevelt, *You Learn by Living* (Louisville: Westminster John Knox Press, 1960), 152.

27. As quoted in John G. Nicolay and John Hay, *Abraham Lincoln: A History*, vol. 2 (New York: Century Co., 1914), 183.

Chapter Three: I Owe $133,000 and Can't Find a Job

1. As quoted in Roger Jaynes, *Al McGuire: The Colorful Warrior* (Champaign, IL: Sports Publishing, 2004), 17.
2. This is a modern restatement of the Greek words of Socrates that appeared in his *Apology*; see, for example, the discussion in Edward Craig, *Routledge Encyclopedia of Philosophy*, vol. 7 (New York: Routledge, 1998), 10.
3. http://dictionary.reference.com/browse/education?s=t. The English word *education* can trace its roots to two Latin words: *educere* (to lead or to bring forth) and *educare* (to rear, to educate). Here, I stress *educere*; see "educate" in *Merriam-Webster's Collegiate Dictionary*, 11th ed.
4. As quoted in David W. DeFord, *1000 Brilliant Achievement Quotes: Advice from the World's Wisest* (Omaha, NE: Ordinary People Can Win, 2004), 119, www.ordinarypeoplecanwin.com.
5. As quoted in Raymond P. Siljander, Jacqueline A. Reina, and Roger A. Siljander, *Literacy Tutoring Handbook* (Springfield, IL: Charles C. Thomas, 2005), 22.
6. Dan Miller, *48 Days to the Work You Love*, rev. ed. (Nashville: B&H Publishing Group, 2010), http://www.48days.com/store.
7. Deborah Arron, *Running from the Law: Why Good Lawyers Are Getting Out of the Legal Profession* (Seattle, WA: Lawyer Avenue Press, 2003).
8. "Running from the Law," http://www.48days.com/2010/10/05/running-from-the-law.
9. http://www.48days.com/48businessideas.
10. "Thoughts from B. C. Forbes," Forbes.com, http://thoughts.forbes.com/thoughts/b-c-forbes?p=4.
11. http://www.48days.com/reading.
12. As quoted in Sidney Sheldon, *The Other Side of Me* (New York: Warner Books, 2005), 240.
13. http://www.48days.com/nmm-cruise.
14. http://donmilleris.com/conference.
15. http://speakitforward.com.
16. http://www.ted.com/pages/registration.
17. http://www.48days.com/liveevents/coaching-with-excellence-live.
18. http://www.willowcreek.com/events/leadership.

19. http://www.48days.com/liveevents/wtb.
20. Oliver Wendell Holmes Sr., *The Autocrat of the Breakfast-Table* (Boston: Houghton Mifflin, 1891), 266, http://books.google.com /books?id=iuG0Zc_GqMwC&dq=autocrat+of+the+breakfast -table&q=man%27s+mind+is+stretched#v=snippet&q=man's%20 mind%20is%20stretched&f=false.
21. http://www.successmagazine.com.
22. http://www.fastcompany.com.
23. http://www.inc.com.
24. http://www.wired.com.
25. http://www.entrepreneur.com.
26. http://www.odemagazine.com.
27. http://www.48days.com.
28. http://blog.guykawasaki.com/#axzz125nNZf6r.
29. http://sethgodin.typepad.com/seths_blog.
30. http://chrisguillebeau.com/3x5.
31. http://www.jonacuff.com/stuffchristianslike.
32. http://michaelhyatt.com.
33. http://freeagentacademy.com.
34. http://wordpress.org.
35. http://www.kiva.org.
36. http://www.worldvision.org.
37. http://www.leavingthecocoon.net/Welcome.html; http://www .men-of-valor.org.
38. Henry Ford, *My Philosophy of Industry and Moving Forward* (Whitefish, MT: Kessinger Publishing, 2005), 89.
39. http://www.toastmasters.org.
40. http://www.dalecarnegie.com.
41. http://www.homeexchange.com; http://www.homclink.org.
42. http://www.vrbo.com.
43. As quoted in Rob Brown, *How to Build Your Reputation: The Secrets of Becoming the "Go to" Professional in a Crowded Marketplace* (Penryn, Cornwall, UK: Ecademy Press, 2007), 31.
44. http://www.globalyouthconnect.org.
45. http://www.akilahinstitute.org/about/partners.
46. http://www.startingbloc.org/ourfellows; http://www.linkedin .com/in/elizabethdearborndavis.
47. TED is a nonprofit devoted to "Ideas Worth Spreading," and TEDx events provide the opportunity for participants to share ideas; http://www.ted.com/tedx; http://www.youtube.com /watch?v=7P_Rr-td7N4.

48. Roy H. Williams, "But *Why* Are You Going to College?" 28 February 2011, Monday Morning Memo, http://www .mondaymorningmemo.com/newsletters/read/1915.

49. Partial list from Kaitlin Madden, "Weird but True: College Degrees," AOL Jobs, 17 February 2011, http://jobs.aol.com /articles/2011/02/17/weird-but-true-college-degrees.

50. B. C. Forbes, *Forbes*, vol. 152, nos. 6–10 (1918): 192, http:// books.google.com/books?id=ZSW8AAAAIAAJ&q=goldstein+ %22he+who+has+learning+without+imagination%22&dq=go ldstein+%22he+who+has+learning+without+imagination%22 &hl=en&sa=X&ei=udtgT7qSCaeQ2QXTm4CGAw&ved=0CDA Q6AEwAA.

51. http://www.blueoctober.com/site.

52. http://keza.com.

53. http://www.gretchenwilson.com/about.html; Luchina Fisher, "Celeb Dropouts Finally Graduate," ABC News, 15 May 2008, http://abcnews.go.com/Entertainment/story?id=4856242&page=2.

54. Daren Fonda and Lisa Scherzer, "10 Things Millionaires Won't Tell You," SmartMoney.com, 11 February 2010, http://www .smartmoney.com/spend/rip-offs/10-things-millionaires-wont -tell-you-23697/?zone=intromessage. These facts and more about wealthy individuals are explored in a book by Jim Taylor, Doug Harrison, and Stephan Kraus, *The New Elite: Inside the Minds of the Truly Wealthy* (New York: AMACOM, 2009).

55. Thomas Stanley and William Danko, *The Millionaire Next Door* (Lanham, MD: Rowan & Littlefield, 1996).

56. Dan Miller, *No More Dreaded Mondays* (New York: Broadway Books, 2008), http://www.48days.com/store.

57. April Rabkin, "Cramming for College at Beijing's Second High," *FastCompany*, 15 August 2011, http://www.fastcompany.com /magazine/158/china-education.

58. As quoted in Garson Kanin, *It Takes a Long Time to Become Young* (New York: Berkley Books, 1979), 139.

Chapter Four: Lemonade Stand or Facebook

1. John Robbins, *Diet for a New America* (Walpole, NH: Stillpoint, 1987); *The Food Revolution* (Berkeley, CA: Conari Press, 2011), 276; "Introduction to The New Good Life," http://www.johnrobbins .info/the-new-good-life/introduction-the-new-good-life.

2. http://www.livingwithed.net/theproduction.asp.

3. http://dictionary.reference.com/browse/poverty; http:// dictionary.reference.com/browse/simplicity?s=t.

4. "We Are the World," http://www.youtube.com /watch?v=k2W4-0qUdHY.

5. http://www.thefreedictionary.com/Swahili; "Swahili Information," http://www.uiowa.edu/~africart/toc/people /Swahili.html.

6. As noted in "Shackleton's Leadership Role," WGBH, http:// main.wgbh.org/imax/shackleton/shackleton.html; about the five thousand respondents, http://www.antarctic-circle.org/advert .htm.

7. As quoted in Janet Lowe, *Welch: An American Icon* (New York: Wiley, 2002), 93.

8. As discussed in Zig Ziglar, *See You at the Top* (Gretna, LA: Pelican, 2000), 313.

9. Helen Keller, *The Open Door* (Garden City, NY: Doubleday, 1957), 17.

10. Roy B. Zuck, *The Speaker's Quote Book*, rev. and expanded ed. (Grand Rapids, MI: Kregel, 2009), 143.

11. http://www.daveramsey.com/fpu/home.

12. http://www.48days.com/48businessideas.

13. http://www.48days.com/category/48-days-podcast.

14. As noted in Jamie Buckingham, *The Last Word (Published and Unpublished)* (Plainfield, NJ: Logos International, 1978), 137.

15. Napoleon Hill and W. Clement Stone, *Success Through a Positive Mental Attitude* (New York: Simon and Schuster, 2007), 83–86.

16. Irvin D. Solomon, *Thomas Edison: The Fort Myers Connection* (Charleston, SC: Arcadia Publishing, 2001), 58.

17. Stephen Covey, *The 7 Habits of Highly Effective People* (New York: Free Press, 2004), 274, 278, 298.

18. http://www.sharkysonthepier.com.

19. Author unknown.

20. http://donmilleris.com/conference.

21. http://speakitforward.com.

22. http://www.chadjeffers.com.

23. http://www.goodreads.com/author/quotes/15321.Confucius.

Chapter Five: Doing Work That Matters

1. These words of Saint Irenaeus are quoted in the Catechism of the Catholic Church, 2nd ed., revised in accordance with the official Latin text promulgated by Pope John Paul II (Vatican City: Libreria Editrice Vaticana, 2000), 77, Article 294; see n139 on that page.

2. Parija B. Kavlianz, "Macy's Cutting 7,000 Jobs," CNNMoney, 2 February 2009, http://money.cnn.com/2009/02/02/news /companies/macys/index.htm; Staff writer, "CBS Profit Rises, But Revenue Declines," RTT News, 2 February 2012, http://www .rttnews.com/1821475/cbs-profit-rises-but-revenue-declines.aspx; Robert Hodierne, "Is There Life After Newspapers?" *American Journalism Review*, February-March 2009, http://ajr.org/Article .asp?id=4679; Ben Fritz, "Blockbuster Files for Chapter 11 Bankruptcy," *Los Angeles Times*, 23 September 2010, http:// latimesblogs.latimes.com/entertainmentnewsbuzz/2010/09 /blockbuster-files-for-chapter-11-bankruptcy-sets-plan-to -reorganize.html.

3. Bureau of Labor Statistics, National Longitudinal Studies, http:// www.bls.gov/nls/nlsfaqs.htm#anch4.

4. Bureau of Labor Statistics, Economic News Release, "Number of Jobs Held, Labor Market Activity, and Earnings Growth Among the Youngest Baby Boomers," 10 September 2010, http://www .bls.gov/news.release/nlsoy.nr0.htm.

5. http://www.stress.org/job.htm.

6. Rich Maloof, "Monday Morning Heart Attacks . . . and Other Health Risks by the Day of the Week," MSN Health, 24 February 2011, http://health.msn.com/health-topics/monday-morning -heart-attacks-and-other-health-risks-by-the-day-of-the-week.

7. Jessica Dickler, "New Year's Resolution: I Quit!" CNNMoney, 23 December 2010, http://money.cnn.com/2010/12/23/pf/workers _want_new_jobs/index.htm.

8. Richard Settersten and Barbara Ray, *Not Quite Adults: Why 20-Somethings Are Choosing a Slower Path to Adulthood* (New York: Bantam Books, 2010), 62.

9. Sara Terry, "Seeking Jobs with Social Value," *Christian Science Monitor*, 27 April 2001, http://www.csmonitor.com/2001/0827 /p16s1-wmwo.html.

10. As quoted in Dick Leatherman, *Is Coffee Break the Best Part of Your Day?: How to Keep Your Job in Today's Turbulent Environment* (Amherst, MA: HRD Press, 2010), 261.

11. http://keza.com.

12. http://iouproject.com.
13. Taylor Wilson, "Bethel University Offers First Scholarships for Bass Fishing," Bassmaster.com, 3 August 2010, http://www .bassmaster.com/news/bethel-university-offers-first-scholarships; Eric Anderson, "The First Woman to Get a College Scholarship in Bass Fishing," PostGame.com, 6 April 2011, http://www .thepostgame.com/features/201104/little-fish-big-pond-story -first-woman-ever-get-college-scholarship-bass-fishing.
14. "2009 College Graduates Moving Back Home in Larger Numbers," Collegegrad.com, http://www.collegegrad.com /press/2009_college_graduates_moving_back_home_in _larger_numbers.shtml.
15. http://www.milkdelivers.org/schools/coaches-corner/sammy -awards; http://www.whymilk.com.
16. "Unusual Scholarships," Scholarships.com, http://www .scholarships.com/financial-aid/college-scholarships /scholarships-by-type/unusual-scholarships/#duckcall.
17. http://www.48days.com/worksheets.
18. For "salt" (Matt. 5:13); and for "light" (Eph. 5:8).
19. Kahlil Gibran, *The Prophet* (New York: Knopf, 2001), 27.
20. Os Guinness, *The Call: Finding and Fulfilling the Central Purpose of Your Life* (Nashville: Thomas Nelson, 2003), 230.
21. As quoted in Edward Mornin and Lorna Mornin, *Saints: A Visual Guide* (Grand Rapids, MI: Eerdmans, 2006), 160.

Chapter Six: Who Are You, and Why Are You Here?

1. Brian Tracy, *Getting Rich in America*, compact discs or MP3 version, http://www.nightingale.com/prod_detail~product~Getting_Rich _America.aspx.
2. http://www.48days.com/worksheets.
3. As quoted in Ann Jordan and Lynne Whaley, *Investigating Your Career* (Mason, OH: Thomson South-Western, 2008), 118.
4. From *Speaker's Sourcebook* by Glenn Van Ekeren (Englewood Cliffs, NJ: Prentice Hall, 1988), 184.
5. From *The Lion King* (1994) presented by Walt Disney Pictures, http://www.imdb.com/title/tt0110357/maindetails; http://www .youtube.com/watch?v=9tmLn6N_Srw.
6. Bronnie Ware, "Regrets of the Dying," Inspirationandchai.com, http://www.inspirationandchai.com/Regrets-of-the-Dying.html.
7. http://www.48days.com/category/48-days-podcast.

8. http://www.inspirationpeak.com/justice.html.

9. As quoted in Zig Ziglar and Ike Reighard, *The One Year Daily Insights* (Carol Stream, IL: Tyndale, 2009), 18, April 18 entry.

10. Frederick Douglass, "History . . . It's Happening," EBSCO Publishing, http://www.ebscohost.com/flashPromo /historyhappenings/fr_douglas.html.

11. Wallace D. Wattles, *The Science of Getting Rich* (New York: Jeremy P. Tarcher/Penguin, 2007); Science of Getting Rich Network, http://www.scienceofgettingrich.net.

12. Napoleon Hill, *Think and Grow Rich* (New York: Tribeca Books, 2011).

13. http://tedyoder.com/fr_home.cfm.

14. The wording of the Liturgy of the Eucharist bears evidence of Jewish prayer at Passover. See Martin K. Barrack, "Our Jewish Heritage," Catholic Education Resource Center, http:// catholiceducation.org/articles/religion/re0002.html; Liturgy of the Eucharist, http://catholic-resources.org/ChurchDocs/Mass.htm.

15. Richard Rohr, *The Naked Now: Learning to See as the Mystics See* (Chestnut Ridge, NY: Crossroad Publishing, 2009), 20, http:// www.cacradicalgrace.org/richard-rohr.

16. Dorothy Sayers, "Why Work?" http://www.faith-at-work.net /Docs/WhyWork.pdf.

17. Mick Jagger as ice-cream salesman, "Before They Were Famous: 12 Celebrity First Jobs," StyleCaster News, 31 March 2010, http://news.stylecaster.com/before-they-were-famous -12-first-jobs; as porter and student, Leslie Ayres, "Celebrity First Jobs: An Omen of Their Future?" Work Goes Strong, 18 January 2011, http://work.lifegoesstrong.com/slideshow /celebrity-first-jobs-omen-their-future-slideshow-image /mick-jagger-going-mental.

18. Floyd Connor, *Hollywood's Most Wanted* (Washington, DC: Brassey's, 2002), 6.

19. Alice Schroeder, *The Snowball: Warren Buffett and the Business of Life* (New York: Bantam Books, 2008), 78, 123.

20. "Ozzy Osbourne: The Prince of Darkness Gets a Book," *Weekend Edition*, NPR, 27 February 2010, http://www.npr .org/2010/02/26/124120813/ozzy-osbourne-the-prince-of -darkness-gets-a-book.

21. Matthew McConaughey biography, http://www.imdb.com /name/nm0000190/bio.

22. Jimmy Stewart Museum, http://www.jimmy.org/biography.

23. Bill Cosby biography, http://www.biography.com/people
/bill-cosby-9258468; http://www.buzzle.com/articles/bill-cosby
-biography.html.
24. Tom Cruise biography, http://www.imdb.com/name
/nm0000129/bio.
25. Tom Phillips, "Chinese University Sets Up Dormitory for
Overprotective Parents," *Metro*, 17 September 2010, http://
www.metro.co.uk/weird/841237-chinese-university-sets-up
-dormitory-for-overprotective-parents.
26. Rachel Rettner, "'Helicopter' Parents Have Neurotic Kids,"
MSNBC, 3 June 2010, http://www.msnbc.msn.com/id/37493795
/ns/health-kids_and_parenting.
27. As quoted in Steve May, *The Story File: 1001 Contemporary
Illustrations* (Peabody, MA: Hendrickson Publishers, 2000), 121.

Chapter Seven: I Asked for Wonder

1. Abraham Joshua Heschel, *I Asked for Wonder: A Spiritual
Anthology*, ed. Samuel H. Dresner (Chestnut Ridge, NY:
Crossroad, 1986), 7.
2. Willard Huntington Wright, *What Nietzsche Taught* (New York:
B. W. Huebsch, 1917), Wright used the pseudonym of S. S. Van
Dine, http://books.google.com/books?id=BfPWAAAAMAAJ
&printsec=frontcover#v=onepage&q=live%20so%20that%20
thou%20mayest&f=false.
3. Numbers 22:21–39, http://www.biblegateway.com/passage
/?search=Numbers%2022:%2021-39&version=NIV.
4. Mark Twain, *The Wit and Wisdom of Mark Twain*, ed. Alex Ayres
(New York: Perennial, 2005), 10, http://books.google.com
/books?id=Ee_aQw6WfK8C&printsec=frontcover#v=onepage
&q=keep%20away%20from%20people&f=false.
5. John Maxwell and Jim Dornan, *Becoming a Person of Influence*
(Nashville: Thomas Nelson, 1997), 126.
6. http://keza.com.
7. Jack Canfield and Janet Switzer, *The Success Principles™: How
to Get From Where You Are to Where You Want to Be* (New York:
HarperCollins, 2005), 189, http://books.google.com/books?id
=UVtcxvx5Zr8C&pg=PA189&dq=timothy+ferriss+%22you+ar
e+the+average+of+the+five+people%22&hl=en&sa=X&ei=Uz
1iT7PRCeiw2wXc8PC0CA&ved=0CEAQ6AEwAQ#v
=onepage&q=timothy%20ferriss%20%22you%20are%20
the%20average%20of%20the%20five%20people%22&f=false.

8. http://www.bodybuilding.com/store/bq/body.html; John Warrillow, "Why Tim Ferriss Sold His Muse," *Inc.*, 11 November 2010, http://www.inc.com/articles/2010/10/why-tim-ferriss-sold -brainquicken.html.

9. http://fourhourworkweek.com.

10. As quoted in Canfield and Switzer, *The Success Principles™*, 190. Mike Murdock is the author of *The Leadership Secrets of Jesus* (Tulsa: Honor Books, 1996), among other books.

11. http://www.markvictorhansen.com/about.php.

12. http://www.48days.com/liveevents/wtb.

13. http://changeyourstars.com.

14. http://bobgoff.com.

15. Tom Waits biography, http://www.imdb.com/name/nm0001823.

16. "*Ubuntu* is a concept that we have in our Bantu languages at home. Ubuntu is the essence of being a person. It means that we are people through other people. We cannot be fully human alone. We are made for interdependence, we are made for family. When you have *ubuntu*, you embrace others. You are generous, compassionate. If the world had more *ubuntu*, we would not have war. We would not have this huge gap between the rich and the poor. You are rich so that you can make up what is lacking for others. You are powerful so that you can help the weak, just as a mother or father helps their children. This is God's dream." Bishop Desmond Tutu, "Desmond Tutu's Recipe for Peace," http://beliefnet.com/Inspiration/2004/04/Desmond-Tutus -Recipe-For-Peace.aspx?p=2.

17. Michael Gelb, *How to Think Like Leonardo da Vinci: Seven Steps to Genius Every Day* (New York: Dell, 1998), 54.

18. http://www.48days.com/2011/01/20/better-death-than-this %E2%80%A6.

19. David M. Ewalt, "Steve Jobs' 2005 Stanford Commencement Address," Forbes.com, 10 May 2011, http://www.forbes.com /sites/davidewalt/2011/10/05/steve-jobs-2005-stanford -commencement-address/3.

20. As quoted in Conrad P. Pritscher, *Einstein & Zen: Learning to Learn* (New York: Peter Lang, 2010), 17.

21. http://www.48days.com.

22. Studies on IQ, " Selected Portions of Intelligence Knowns and Unknowns," report of a task force established by the Board of Scientific Affairs, American Psychological Association, 7 August

1995, http://webspace.ship.edu/cgboer/iku.html; studies on creativity; Po Bronson and Ashley Merryman, "The Creativity Crisis," *Newsweek*, 10 July 2010, http://www.thedailybeast.com /newsweek/2010/07/10/the-creativity-crisis.html.

23. For all of the lyrics, go to http://www.cowboylyrics.com/lyrics /lonestar/unusually-unusual-6859.html.

24. Thomas Stanley, *The Millionaire Mind* (Kansas City, MO: Andrews McMeel, 2001), 99–100.

25. T. E. Lawrence, *Seven Pillars of Wisdom* (Chatham, Kent, UK: Wordsworth Editions Limited, 1997), 7.

26. As quoted in Robert K. Greenleaf, *Creating and Changing Mindsets, Movies of the Mind* (Newfield, ME: Greenleaf Papanek Publications, 2005), 45.

27. As quoted in Peter H. Thomas, *LifeManual* (Scottsdale, AZ: LifePilot, 2005), 124, http://books.google.com/books?id=b4Le mkSrHNAC&pg=PA124&dq=brian+tracy+%22+all+successfu l+men+and+women%22&hl=en&sa=X&ei=Yz1jT-D4MeWW2 AXYrNTRCA&ved=0CFYQ6AEwBA#v=onepage&q=brian%20 tracy%20%22%20all%20successful%20men%20and%20 women%22&f=false.

28. Carl Sandburg, "Washington Monument by Night," in *Slabs of the Sunburnt West* (New York: Harcourt, Brace, 1922), 18, stanza 4.

29. Langston Hughes, *The Collected Poems of Langston Hughes*, ed. Arnold Rampersad (New York: Vintage Books, 1995), 32.

30. As quoted by Brennan Manning, *The Ragamuffin Gospel* (Sisters, OR: Multnomah, 2000), 185–86, emphasis added.

31. Bill Gates Sr., *Showing Up for Life* (New York: Random House, 2009), 77.

32. Ibid., 78.

33. Bill Gates biography, http://www.biography.com/people /bill-gates-9307520.

34. William H. Danforth, *I Dare You!* (1941; repr. Whitefish, MT: Kessinger Publishing, 2003), 51–52, emphasis added.

35. Ibid., 52, emphasis added.

36. As quoted in Harold R. McAlindon, *The Little Book of Big Ideas: Inspiration, Encouragement, and Tips to Stimulate Creativity and Improve Your Life* (Nashville: Cumberland House Publishing, 1999), 31.

37. Danforth, *I Dare You!*, 52.

38. As quoted in McAlindon, *The Little Book of Big Ideas*, 15.

39. http://jaredangaza.com.
40. http://www.bartleby.com/348/authors/422.html.
41. *The Pursuit of Happyness* (2006), Sony Pictures, http://www .sonypictures.com/homevideo/thepursuitofhappyness/; Chris Gardner, "Do What You Dream," *AARP The Magazine*, 17 February 2011, http://www.aarp.org/personal-growth/life -stories/info-02-2011/do-what-you-dream.html.
42. *Braveheart* (1995), Icon Entertainment International, http:// www.imdb.com/title/tt0112573/quotes.
43. As quoted in Donna VanLiere, *Finding Grace* (New York: St. Martin's, 2009), 173, http://books.google.com/books?id=kkp s2pfA2B0C&pg=PA173&dq=c+s+lewis+why+love+if+losin g+hurts+so+much&hl=en&sa=X&ei=TUtjT8fDIYSNsAKm 37mcCw&ved=0CEsQ6AEwAw#v=onepage&q=c%20s%20 lewis%20why%20love%20if%20losing%20hurts%20so%20 much&f=false.
44. Salman Akhtar, "'Someday . . .' and 'If Only . . .' Fantasies" (paper, conference on borderline states, University of Paris, 5–6 November 1994). Akhtar is professor of psychiatry at Jefferson Medical College, Philadelphia. Go to http://www.pep-web.org /document.php?id=apa.044.0723a.
45. Marcel Proust biographical summary, *Guardian* (UK), 22 July 2008, http://www.guardian.co.uk/books/2008/jun/11 /marcelproust.

Chapter Eight: Not (Only) for Profit

1. http://givingpledge.org.
2. Jim Collins, *Good to Great* (New York: HarperCollins, 2001). Collins notes the three components in excerpts from his monograph, *Good to Great and the Social Sectors* (New York: HarperCollins, 2005), on this site: http://www.jimcollins.com /books/g2g-ss.html.
3. Nancy Lublin, "Why Charities Should Have an Expiration Date," Fast Company, 8 December 2010, http://www.fastcompany.com /magazine/151/do-something-why-charities-should-die.html.
4. http://www.nonprofitreporter.org/about.html; Rob Reich, "New Research on 501c3s: Anything Goes: Approval of Nonprofit Status by the IRS," Stanford University, http://www .stanford.edu/group/reichresearch/cgi-bin/site/2009/12/05 /new-research-on-501c3s-anything-goes-approval-of-nonprofit -status-by-the-irs.

5. Carol Tice, "Starting a Nonprofit Business," Entrepreneur
.com, 1 December 2006, http://www.entrepreneur.com
/article/170776.

6. http://www.48days.net/forum/topics/profiting-from-a-christian.

7. http://www.terracycle.net/en-US.

8. Randy Pausch, *The Last Lecture* (New York: Hyperion, 2008),
132–33.

9. http://www.charitywater.org; http://www.invisiblechildren.com.

10. http://vimeo.com/28104222.

11. Blake Mycoskie, *Start Something That Matters* (New York,
Spiegel and Grau, 2011).

12. http://puravidacreategood.com/pvcg_index.php.

13. Excerpt from *Dumb and Dumber* (1994), New Line Cinema,
http://www.youtube.com/watch?v=gqdNe8u-Jsg.

Chapter Nine: Retirement: The American Dream?

1. As quoted in Matt Weinstein and Luke Barber, *Gently Down the
Stream: 4 Unforgettable Keys to Success* (New York: Perigee Books,
2006), 130.

2. Thomas Stanley, *The Millionaire Mind* (Kansas City, MO:
Andrews McMeel, 2001), 186.

3. Leo Tolstoy, *My Confession, My Religion: The Gospel in Brief*
(Rockville, MD: Wildside Press, 2010), 232.

4. As quoted in Jack Canfield and Janet Switzer, *The Success
Principles™: How to Get from Where You Are to Where You Want
to Be* (New York: HarperCollins, 2005), 425.

5. Tom Wilson was the creator of Ziggy, http://www.goodreads
.com/author/quotes/68214.Tom_Wilson.

6. Jane Kallir et al., *Grandma Moses in the 21st Century*
(Alexandria, VA: Art Services International, 2001), 52; Grandma
Moses wrote her autobiography, *My Life's History* (New York:
Harper and Brothers, 1952). Her name was Anna Mary Moses.

7. As quoted in James Geary, *Geary's Guide to the World's Great
Aphorists* (New York: Bloomsbury USA, 2007), 85, http://books
.google.com/books?id=6ttxTZ-v9RUC&printsec=frontcover#v
=onepage&q=what%20lies%20behind%20us&f=false.

8. Author unknown. Many versions have appeared over many
years. This one is sometimes attributed to Nadine Stair, age
eighty-five; http://www.devpsy.org/nonscience/daisies.

9. Whitney Self, "Little Jimmy Dickens Celebrates His 90th Birthday in Downtown Nashville," CMT.com, 20 January 2011, http://www.cmt.com/news/country-music/1656348 /little-jimmy-dickens-celebrates-his-90th-birthday-in -downtown-nashville.jhtml.

10. As quoted in Hal Green, "Showing Mercy Is Your Choice," *Muscatine Journal*, 24 February 2010, http://muscatinejournal .com/news/opinion/columns/article_9ad65c78-2162-11df-a6f6 -001cc4c002e0.html.

11. Henry David Thoreau, *Walden: or, Life in the Woods* (Boston: Houghton Mifflin, 1893), 143, http://books.google.com /books?id=ia_NRtTcT74C&printsec=frontcover#v=onepage&q =went%20to%20the%20woods&f=false.

12. Ibid., 143–44, emphasis in original.

13. As quoted in "Frozen in Time," *Manila Bulletin*, 5 September 2004, http://www.mb.com.ph/node/178048.

Chapter Ten: I Have a Feeling We're Not in Kansas Anymore

1. William Shakespeare, *Hamlet*, act 2, scene 2, line 254.

2. See Jack Canfield and Mark Victor Hansen, *Chicken Soup for the Soul* (Deerfield Beach, FL: HCI, 2001), 285–86.

3. As quoted in Jeffrey Harris, *Transformative Entrepreneurs: How Walt Disney, Steve Jobs, Muhammad Yunus, and Other Innovators Succeeded* (New York: Palgrave Macmillan, 2012), 89, http:// books.google.com/books?id=7GetAzYB70oC&pg=PA89&dq= henry+ford+%22failure+is+simply+the+opportunity+to+begin +again&hl=en&sa=X&ei=6JhjT5WSF-bW2gXQwcjSCQ&ved= 0CDUQ6AEwAQ#v=onepage&q=henry%20ford%20 %22failure%20is%20simply%20the%20opportunity%20to%20 begin%20again&f=false.

4. Dan Malachowski, "Wasted Time at Work Costing Companies Billions," *San Francisco Chronicle*, 11 July 2005, http://www .sfgate.com/cgi-bin/article.cgi?f=/g/a/2005/07/11/wastingtime .TMP&ao=all.

5. Ibid.

6. Kate Lister, "How Many People Actually Telecommute?" WorkShifting.com, 21 February 2010, http://www.workshifting .com/2010/02/how-many-people-actually-telecommute.html; "How Many People Telecommute?" Telework Research Network,

http://www.teleworkresearchnetwork.com/research
/people-telecommute.

7. Michelle Conlin, "Smashing the Clock," *BloombergBusinessweek*,
11 December 2006, http://www.businessweek.com/magazine
/content/06_50/b4013001.htm.

8. Ibid.

9. Ibid.

10. Chuck Salter "Calling JetBlue," *Fast Company*, 19 December
2009, http://www.fastcompany.com/magazine/82/jetblue
_agents.html.

11. http://en.wikipedia.org/wiki/Coworking. See also Kerry
Miller, "Where the Coffee Shop Meets the Cubicle,"
BloombergBusinessweek, 26 February 2007, http://www
.businessweek.com/smallbiz/content/feb2007
/sb20070226_761145.htm.

12. http://wiki.coworking.info/w/page/16583831/FrontPage.

13. I've never been able to identify an author for this story. I have
taken the liberty to modify it over the years.

14. Roger von Oech, *A Whack on the Side of the Head* (New York:
Warner Books 1998), 144.

15. Joanne Long, "Charles Dickens," Vassar Special Collections,
http://specialcollections.vassar.edu/exhibits/dickens/long.html;
Charles Dickens, *The Writings of Charles Dickens: Sketches by Boz*
(Boston: Houghton Mifflin, 1894), ix–x, http://books.google
.com/books?id=gfM0AAAAMAAJ&pg=PR10&dq=writings+of
+charles+dickens+no+return+in+money&hl=en&sa=X&ei=
-uBlT_zMG6fg2QXMx-zaCA&ved=0CDsQ6AEwAA#v=onepag
e&q&f=false.

16. John Maxwell, *Talent Is Never Enough* (Nashville: Thomas
Nelson, 2007), 107.

17. Malcolm Gladwell, *Outliers* (New York: Little Brown, 2008), see
especially chapter 2 about 10,000 hours.

18. If you want to join the lively discussion about this topic,
jump in here. Go to www.48days.com and search for "Put in
10,000 Hours—Then We'll Talk," http://www.48days
.com/2011/09/27/put-in-10000-hours
-%E2%80%93-then-we%E2%80%99ll-talk.

About the Authors

Dan Miller, president of 48 Days, specializes in creative thinking for increased personal and business success. He is the author of the widely acclaimed *48 Days to the Work You Love* and *No More Dreaded Mondays*. He writes for many popular magazines and web portals; has been a guest on CBS, MSNBC, *The 700 Club*, and the *The Dave Ramsey Show*; and appears frequently on popular radio programs. Dan has been happily married to Joanne for more than forty-four years. For articles and free resources, visit www.48Days.com.

Jared Angaza is a branding consultant, philanthropist, and blogger. He's the founder of KEZA, an ethical fashion company, and Angaza Consulting. Jared consults primarily on the issues of gender equality, business development, and rebranding Africa. He is currently helping to rebrand one of Kenya's premier coffee companies. Jared and his wife, Ilea, have lived and operated in East Africa since March 2006, consulting NGOs, governments, individuals, and businesses to transform their work into soul-filled art. Check on current activities at www.jaredangaza.com.